COMPARATIVE LEGISLATURES

PRENTICE-HALL
CONTEMPORARY COMPARATIVE POLITICS SERIES
JOSEPH LaPALOMBARA, Editor

J. BLONDEL

University of Essex

Prentice-Hall, Inc.,
Englewood Cliffs, N.J.

COMPARATIVE
LEGISLATURES

Library of Congress Cataloging in Publication Data

Blondel, Jean.
    Comparative legislatures.

    (Contemporary comparative politics series)
    Bibliography: p.
    1. Legislative bodies.   I. Title.
JF501.B56   328'.3   73-1867
ISBN   0-13-153874-8
ISBN   0-13-153866-7 (pbk)

COMPARATIVE LEGISLATURES
J. Blondel

Printed in the United States of America

10   9   8   7   6   5   4   3   2   1

PRENTICE-HALL INTERNATIONAL, INC., London
PRENTICE-HALL OF AUSTRALIA, PTY. LTD., Sydney
PRENTICE-HALL OF CANADA, LTD., Toronto
PRENTICE-HALL OF INDIA PRIVATE LIMITED, New Delhi
PRENTICE-HALL OF JAPAN, INC., Tokyo

CONTENTS

FOREWORD

The organization of the Contemporary Comparative Politics Series is based on a number of assumptions and guidelines that are worth calling to the reader's attention. Foremost among these is that the undergraduate student of comparative politics is less interested in political science than we might hope, but more capable of synthetic analysis than we may imagine. If this is so, then it would be an enormous mistake to pretend to organize an introductory series around one or more half-baked "theories" of politics or political systems—theories that are difficult for even the more hardened members of the profession to digest. It would seem equally debatable whether the undergraduate student has a strong desire to learn in depth the institutional arrangements and workings of any single political system, whether that system be as established as that of Great Britain or as new and exotic as that of Tanzania.

What, then, can we expect of those undergraduates who study comparative politics? First, I think that they are quickly turned off by simplistic or spurious efforts to lend the discipline a theoretical elegance it manifestly does not possess; second, that saturation treatments of single political systems are as unpalatable today when the countries are individually packaged as they were when several countries appeared between the same hard covers; third, that the undergraduates sitting in our classrooms might very well be turned on if they learned what sorts of things political scientists do and what kinds of knowledge of the political process they can glean from the things we do. These things, incidentally, would involve not merely data-gathering on some aspect of the political system, but also speculative and normative considerations about the relationship between politics and the good life. We can expect that if the things to be written and lectured about are carefully chosen and intelligently organized, the undergraduate will display a striking capacity to synthesize information and to develop skills in analyzing political phenomena at least as impressive as, say, those of a New York taxi driver, a voluble parent, or a political orator.

Another major assumption underlying the organization of the series is that the topics included should not reflect a commitment to an institutional or behavioral, normative or empirical approach. If members of the profession are still battling about such things, let them spare undergraduates the arid, scholastic, and essentially unproductive nature of such encounters. The authors of this series are neither bare-facts empiricists nor "cloud-ninety" political moralists; they neither sanctify nor abominate institutional or behavioral analysis, but would rather use whatever methods are available to enlighten the reader about important aspects of political life. To emphasize the important is also to be relevant, and our correlative assumption here is that the student who wants political science to be "relevant" does not mean by this that it should be banal, simple-minded, or unsystematic.

Since no series can tell us everything about politics, we have had to choose what we consider to be the important, relevant, and reasonably integrated topics. Such choices are always arbitrary to some extent. However, we have sought to accord attention to certain standards and ubiquitous institutions as well as to newer conceptual and analytical foci that have provoked a good deal of recent research and discussion. Thus, the series will have a volume on Comparative Legal Cultures, but another on Comparative Political Violence; it will include a fine volume on Constitutionalism and one on Revolutionary Movements.

In this short volume, Jean Blondel takes an important step in providing us with data and analysis of legislative bodies within a framework that is genuinely comparative. This is no mean achievement in view of the paucity of even the most elementary information we may wish to have about legislative bodies. The data Professor Blondel has collected, and his creative use of them, underscore the need for producing even greater amounts of descriptive information.

More important in this volume, however, are Blondel's analytical chapters. Rather than echo the growing chorus of concern over the alleged decline of legislatures, he offers us some fresh insights into the varying roles that legislatures and their members can fill in politics. In doing so, it is particularly striking that he manages to bridge East-West, democratic-totalitarian, and other barriers that sometimes inhibit effective comparative analysis. His discussion of the significance and probable future of legislatures takes on particularly interesting implications because of this.

Volumes to follow this one will represent what we believe is an interesting and useful mosaic that should be appealing to those who teach, those who learn about, and all of those who try to understand politics.

JOSEPH LaPALOMBARA

New Haven

PREFACE

After a long eclipse, the study of legislatures once more attracted the attention of political scientists at the end of the 1960s. It is no longer fashionable to argue that everything is decided by governments in the secret of Cabinets or by parties in the confines of national committees. A more realistic appraisal of the ideas of influence and power has led to the recognition that, though the constitutional rights of legislatures may be very large, their strength may vary in a whole variety of ways and through many different techniques. Indeed, this welcome development concerns not only legislatures, but also other structures of government, such as bureaucracies, local authorities, judiciaries, and the executives themselves. Too little attention had been given to such institutions in the past, for the main research effort was directed to mass electorates, interest groups, or parties. Perhaps this new interest in analyzing and understanding political power will force a more systematic analysis of the types of influence and authority that are at the root of the role played by legislatures and other governmental structures in all political systems.

This book is intended to be a contribution to the revival of studies of legislatures. Because legislatures had been ignored for so long, much is still unknown about the activities and effect of representative assemblies. For most of the new countries, data are hard to find and patchy in the extreme; even for older countries, studies of outcomes of legislatures, of their influence in both important and routine matters, of the attitudes and desires of their members are merely beginning to emerge. A truly worldwide comparative study is, therefore, difficult to undertake. Yet only by looking at legislatures comparatively, by trying to rank their achievements and examine the impact of various types of political and socioeconomic systems on their development and effectiveness, can we come to a comprehensive assessment of their role and their potential. In the last analysis, we need to be able to know what assemblies can do and cannot do, what they can do best, and under what conditions these achievements can occur. But if this is to be done, it has to be done comparatively, and on a worldwide basis. We shall, therefore, look at legislatures on the widest possible plane, trying, as far as possible, to make the assessment comprehensive and to take into account at least a representative section of all political systems.

Because of lack of existing material, we have had to use two types of sources in the preparation of this work. For a large part, in particular for the study of Western countries, we have relied mainly on published sources; for new countries, except in the case of a small number of countries for which pioneering studies have been published, we have relied on the analysis of the activities of legislatures themselves through debates and other official publications. This study, therefore, would not have been possible if it had not been for the help given by the Institute of Commonwealth Studies, in London, the foreign documentation section of the French National Assembly in Paris, the Interparliamentary Union in Geneva, as well as the Secretariat of the legislatures of the Netherlands, the German Democratic Republic, Tunisia, Singapore, West Samoa, and Uruguay, all of which I wish particularly to thank here; I also wish to thank Dr. J. Biehl of the Catholic University of Valparaiso and Dr. O. Arias of the University of Costa Rica for their help in forwarding documents and debates, as well as Mrs. N. Libeskind, Mr. A. Baccouche, and Mr. H. Blanco for having assisted me in this research. Above all, I wish to thank Professor J. LaPalombara of Yale University for having encouraged me to undertake this project and for having helped to improve the manuscript in a major way. I hope that, despite its limitations, this study will help to stimulate further work on legislatures, both individually and comparatively and that it will be seen less as a stock-taking of prior findings than as a primer for future inquiries.

J. Blondel

Colchester, Essex, England

COMPARATIVE LEGISLATURES

THE
PROBLEM
OF
LEGISLATURES

1

Legislatures (or assemblies, or parliaments) pose perhaps the most fascinating problem of all structures of government, for they have been and continue to be both the most decried and the most revered, the most hoped for and often the least successful institution in contemporary governments. One finds legislatures in liberal and authoritarian governments, though of course not in all of the latter; and in both systems the legislature is often held to be a "rubber stamp." From the late eighteenth century, when the strengthening of powers of the legislatures in England, America, and France was expected to provide a form of liberal rule and even democratic government, the story of legislatures has been one of ups and downs, of great expectations and almost total abjection. Indeed, a century before, as soon as the British Parliament started affirming its rights, under Charles I, it came under the domination of the "Protector" and ceased being effective; a hundred and fifty years later, in 1789, it took only four years for the French National Assembly to move from an ambitious assertion of its powers to a position of silence and fear. After the Napoleonic wars, legislatures began to multiply throughout Western Europe, but their history was often unhappy: authoritarian governments suppressed them or reduced their rights and sometimes succeeded, as in France in the 1850s, to silence them by almost totalitarian methods, all the while maintaining them alive in conditions of abject impotence. And in the twentieth century, first in the European dictatorial regimes of the interwar years, and later in many parts of Africa, Asia, and Latin America (where, indeed, legislatures had a long history of troubles, with an occasional resurgeance between periods of limited or no independence), legislatures often became mere puppets, exercising little influence, meeting very rarely, and showing few signs of even moving toward greater activity in those instances when they were not simply abolished by military rulers. Yet the idea of a legislature survived and continued to be, even in the most authoritarian governments, a symbol of "democracy" and popular sovereignty.

Legislatures are rarely "strong." Even in "liberal democracies" many complain about their impotence, their decline, their ineffectiveness; and if they are strong, they are often blamed for their inconsistency, their squabbles, and thus the same ineffectiveness. On the other hand, they are rarely abolished for very long: one prefers a subservient legislature to no legislature. Pessimists cannot help noting their resilience, their somewhat miraculous powers of regeneration, their curious will to survive. When asked after the Terror, in 1795, what had happened to him, a well-known French politician said simply "I survived." The French legislature also "survived" in the same fashion, as legislatures in many countries of the contemporary world have done. Even if, as in many cases, there were periods of interruption, the symbol has survived, has made most authoritarian governments wary about the absence of a legislature, and often has led to the legislature's rebirth.

This, then, is the problem. How has an institution which is supposed to promote liberalism and democracy achieved apparently so little in the very countries in which liberalism is held to prevail? Why is the literature on the British, French, and American legislatures so full of complaints about inefficiency or uselessness? Why are legislatures apparently so maladjusted to the very thing which they are supposed to do? Conversely, why are legislatures so resilient even where they are clamped down? Are they or are they not appropriate to "liberalism" and "democracy"? Are they an unwieldy instrument, when left to work out freely the conditions of political life? Are they indecisive by their very nature and have they to be, not merely led, but in fact controlled and constantly guided?

Before we begin to explore the characteristics of legislatures and the extent or limits of their real influence, we need to examine a little more closely the nature of the problem and the causes of the paradox. If legislatures are often both so weak and so resilient, is it not because something went wrong, somewhere, in the adaptation of an idea, or an ideal, to the reality? Legislatures stemmed from the concept of representation, a concept which generated a number of theories about what legislatures should do or had to do. Although we cannot attempt to narrate the history of legislatures here, we should at least see how far the reality met the expectation.

**THE ORIGINAL
BLUEPRINT:
LEGISLATURES
AND LAWMAKING**

At the risk of oversimplifying—and we shall have occasion to examine this point more carefully in Chapter 2—it can be said that the real nature of the difficulty arose from a simple but fundamental misunderstanding. From the theorists of the seventeenth century to those of the contemporary world, it has been held as axiomatic (and indeed the point was demonstrated logically by Locke) that the function of legislaturers was to make laws—i.e., to pass the most general rules under which countries were to be governed.[1] The argument is as follows: if the "people" are to be sovereign, or at least as powerful as possible, their representatives should be concerned primarily with the most general rules. Executives are needed to keep the country going, but legislatures could and should decide on the general rules.

This conception appeared to be logical and seemed to tie liberal government (and later democracy) to the existence of healthy and lively legislatures. Admittedly, two problems remained. The first related to the relationship between the representative principle and the ideals of liberalism and democracy. As the people were seemingly too numerous and not competent enough to deliberate, it struck theorists as both reasonable and inevitable to entrust a much smaller group with the duty to act on their behalf. Representative government stands halfway between no control of the executive by the people and complete control of the destinies of the country by the people themselves. It follows that governments which want to bypass or curb the legislature may justify doing so by claiming that such action *increases* democracy. By appealing directly to the people, they allege that they are following more closely the principles of popular sovereignty than the supporters of legislatures and representative government.

The second problem related to the notion of "general rules," which remained vague and ill-defined. Supporters of the idea of representative government felt that some line would have to be drawn between matters to be dealt with by the legislature and matters to be left to the executive. But the distinction between general rules and special bills is difficult to draw in practice. Insofar as the borderline remained vague, executives were prone to interfere in a variety of circumstances. In particular, whenever there was a question of urgency, which Locke held to be the prime criterion for distinguishing between legislative and executive fields, executive intervention could be justified in areas which might otherwise be described as "general." [2]

---

[1] John Locke, *Second Treatise on Civil Government*, Chapter XI. Also Montesquieu, *Spirit of Laws*, Book XI, Chapter 6.

[2] Locke, *op. cit.*, Chapter XII.

Despite these difficulties, it was at least arguable that the development of legislatures would help the development of liberal and democratic government. It would help liberal government because the executive would be constrained to act only in conformity with the decisions of the legislature and therefore would not be despotic or even authoritarian. It would help democratic government because, if the legislature were elected by and representative of the people as a whole, the general rules it established presumably would be the product of the collective thinking of men who had the confidence of the people. It even seemed that a legislature organized along these lines would constitute both a necessary and a sufficient condition for liberalism and democracy, for once the idea of *direct* popular government was rejected as impractical, representative assemblies were the only known device by which executives could be restrained (liberalism) and restrained on the basis of the people's will (democracy).

THE DECLINE OF LEGISLATURES

Not unnaturally, disappointment with legislatures was very high when legislatures proved unable to bring about liberalism or democracy. It is possible to distinguish three forms of this disappointment, which do not necessarily correspond to chronological developments. The first can be summarized in the expression of Bryce about the "decline of legislatures." [3] As we noted earlier, assemblies had become subservient during the French Revolution. But in the first decades of the nineteenth century legislatures had been revitalized. Later, however, a decline seemed to set it. In his classic study of European governments of the turn of the century, Lowell examined with some distress the characteristics of legislatures in France, Italy, Germany, Austro-Hungary, and Switzerland, and noted a number of ways in which the reality did not fit the blueprint; [4] Bryce echoed many of these points in his study of the American Commonwealth.[5]

The indictment of *members* of assemblies was combined with the criticisms of pressure put by the executive. Feelings of national unity were not sufficient in Italy; the complications and constraints resulting from pressure of the Slav nationalities unduly restricted representatives of Hungarian constituencies; British MPs seemed to have lost their will to legislate; [6]

[3] Lord Bryce, *Modern Democracies* (London: Macmillan & Co., Ltd., 1921), I, 367–77, Chapter 58.

[4] A. B. Lowell, *Governments and Parties in Continental Europe* (Cambridge: Harvard University Press, 1896).

[5] Lord Bryce, *The American Commonwealth* (London: Macmillan & Co., Ltd., 1888), I, 165–232. Cf. p. 193: "Legislation on public matters is scanty in quantity and generally mediocre in quality."

[6] A. B. Lowell, *op. cit.*, I, 156 ff.

American congressmen seemed to be content with low quality in the laws which they passed. Deals, arrangements, careerism, and other unfortunate happenings led Bryce and Lowell to believe that the institution of the legislature was, to a large extent, mined from the inside. Quite probably, and indeed almost certainly, the situation was no better in the unreformed British Parliament or the French Chambers of the pre-1848 period; but for these earlier periods, analysis was lacking.[7] Despite their failings, however, assemblies spread to almost the whole of Europe and Latin America throughout the nineteenth century, and their spread seemed to be coupled with disillusionment about their political effectiveness, not so much any longer because of executive despotism as because of their own failings and the failings of their members.

With the period between the two world wars began a second type of disillusionment arising from the development of "rubber-stamp" assemblies. The emergence of the Soviet Union and of other dictatorships in Europe started a mode of political life in which assemblies became mere parodies of deliberative bodies. However weak the German Reichstag had been under Bismarck, it did debate matters and managed to embarrass the government in some situations. But Hitler's Reichstag, like Mussolini's, Salazar's, and Stalin's legislatures, seemed to be the last step before the total demise of parliaments. Such "rubber-stamp" legislatures no longer seemed worthy of attention.

The disappearance of some dictatorships after World War II did not lead to a corresponding reduction in the number and percentage of "rubber-stamp" assemblies. In Eastern European states first, and later in many new states, particularly in Africa, legislatures were reduced to little more than decorative institutions. In the Third World some new countries, such as India and Ceylon, gave their legislatures a semblance of life. But Latin American assemblies continued to have a checkered history. Some traditional states in the Middle East created legislatures, but they often resembled those of the Central European states of the 1880s. And with Ghana, Egypt, and Guinea, "progressive" Third World regimes showed that they, too, could have legislatures which were no more than rubber stamps. Their model was reproduced, to varying degrees, in many of the new states of the 1960s.

Thirdly, in the postwar years, legislatures of Western European states often seemed to become increasingly streamlined and increasingly confined to obeying the fiats of strong executives backed by a disciplined party. In Britain, Germany, and Sweden the members' initiative was not markedly

---

[7] The question was nonetheless envisaged by Bryce: "Yet the House of Commons seems to hold a slightly lower place in the esteem of the people than it did in the days of Melbourne, and Peel. Its intellectual quality has not risen. Its proceedings are less fully reported." (*op. cit.*, p. 370).

greater than in the Austrian or German legislatures of the pre-1914 period. The French legislature, which had long been more independent, succumbed because of its very individualism to the "streamlining" of de Gaulle's 1958 constitution.[8] Thus European assemblies appeared to have suffered a further decline, due perhaps to the very inadequacies which Bryce and Lowell had described. Unlike parts of the Third World, which had rubber-stamp legislatures, Western regimes remained liberal and democratic, parties could and did compete, and elections had a real meaning. But the executive's upper hand seemed to have become so strong that assemblies appeared on the verge of becoming mere decorative organs despite longer sittings and debates.

Even the exceptions, however prestigious, such as the American Congress, seemed to become increasingly rare. In some cases—e.g., France, as we have seen already—the legislatures fell victim to "streamlining." In Pakistan, Indonesia, and Brazil, assemblies which had behaved "too" independently suddenly lost their inability to behave in a concerted fashion, and with this loss they lost their power. For a few months, in Congo-Brazzaville, the assembly seemed omnipotent, but it fell very quickly. Even in the United States, the negative character of Congress led to much impatience; it seemed that only the decentralized structure of the country could justify the waste and procrastination that characterized the American legislature in many of its moves, and Congress was often bypassed by executive or judicial action. Whether or not legislatures had declined in quality in the nineteenth century, in the twentieth they were gradually reduced to minor or even negligible roles.

THE RESILIENCE OF LEGISLATURES

Why is it, then, that most newly formed states create legislatures, and why, in the large majority of cases, do states which dispense with their legislatures quickly create assemblies? Of the 138 countries which exist in the world today, only five, all in the Middle East, have never had a legislature. Four of these states have traditional "absolutist" regimes and the fifth, Yemen, moved from an absolutist system to a "progressive" republic form of government without transition. There are other traditional states in which a monarch still plays a large part in the government, but they do have legislatures even if, as in Tudor or Stuart England, these bodies have few powers and little authority. In 1971, eleven states fit in this category, though variations exist from Bhutan to Iran and from Kuwait to Laos.[9]

Indeed, it is among the "progressive" or "modernizing" states that one

---

[8] A. B. Lowell, *op. cit.*, I, 156 ff.

[9] See Appendix I for details on the characteristics of countries and their assemblies.

often finds a greater propensity to dispense with the assembly. In early 1971, thirty states had no assembly, though in four of them an assembly was in the process of formation (Bolivia, Pakistan, Upper Volta, Morocco). And the position was somewhat ambiguous in a further two, Lesotho and Panama.[10] These States divide fairly evenly between "left," "center" and "right." At least ten of the states without assemblies can be described as progressive in their social and economic policies (Algeria, Cuba, Iraq, Mali, Peru, Somalia, Sudan, Syria, South Yemen, and Bolivia[11]); eight occupy a center position or are very difficult to classify but probably should not be labeled as outright conservative (Burma, Burundi, Central African Republic, Congo, Dahomey, Togo, Yemen and Zaïre); and, alongside the four absolutist countries mentioned above, four conservative regimes do not have assemblies, though in all of these cases the absence of legislatures seems purely temporary (Argentina, Greece, Nigeria, and Uganda). Thus legislatures exist very broadly across the world. While older and richer countries are more likely to have assemblies, these are also present in most of the poorer countries and in most of the newer polities.

Nor is there in any real sense a long-term decline in the percentage of states without assemblies—a fact which would suggest that executives are unable to dispense with these "useless" institutions. Admittedly, in the late 1960s the percentage of states without legislatures did show some increase (Figure 1–1), but the analysis by geographical area gives the explanation. Of six geographical areas (Atlantic, Eastern European and North Asian Communist, Middle East and North Africa, South and Southeast Asia, Africa South of the Sahara, and Central and South America), five have remained stable over the postwar period. The percentage of states with assemblies is very high in the Atlantic and Communist area (95 percent); in the Middle East it has been consistently low (50–60 percent); and in Latin America and Asia it is intermediate (80–90 percent). Only in Africa did the percentage decline from a high—95 percent—at the time when most of the countries acquired independence (around 1960) to an apparently stable 70 percent in the late 1960s. This drop was to be expected: by comparison with Latin America and Asia, the percentage of African states which had legislatures was probably accidentally high as a result of the conditions under which independence was granted. The current African percentage seems normal, inasmuch as it stands about halfway between that achieved

---

[10] Elections took place in the middle of 1971 in Indonesia, for the first time since 1955; the Pakistan constituent assembly was suspended as a result of the East Pakistan revolt; the Lesotho and Panama situations remained confused as a result of coups.

[11] A "popular assembly" was created in 1971 in Bolivia, but it was provisional and was soon dismissed by a further coup.

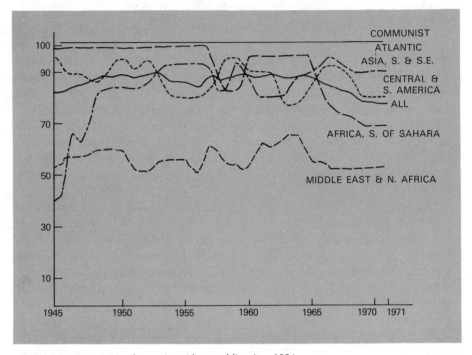

Figure 1–1   Percentage of countries with assemblies since 1954.

by Middle Eastern countries and that achieved by the rest of the Third World. Current developments simply do not show any trend toward the total demise of the legislature idea.

Legislatures are thus spread very broadly across the whole world. Furthermore, few states appear to remain very long without one. The absence of a legislature seems in almost all cases to be a temporary occurrence, either deliberately so (as when a legislature is abolished because of instability or the need to reform the institution—e.g., in the cases of Turkey or Ghana in the past) or because leaders seem unable to maintain themselves in office for long without the legitimizing influence of a legislature—e.g., the cases of Upper Volta, Indonesia, Pakistan, even South Yemen, and possibly Syria in the early 1970s. Very few countries—Cuba, Burma, Syria, and Iraq are the only four cases—have remained for a whole decade without a legislature. Some sort of natural law seems to force leaders of modern politics sooner or later to create legislatures or to be overthrown and replaced by new men who will, in turn, create an assembly. The idea of the legislature is thus inherently resilient, Castro being perhaps the only leader who aggressively rejects the notion of a legislature.

Despite their decline, despite the fact that they may often be seen as rubber stamps, legislatures not only survive but are revived in most of the countries from which they had disappeared. Thus the qeustion is probably not as simple as might seem at first. Short-term movements must be distinguished from long-term changes: in Latin America there have been periodic suppressions of the legislatures in some of the countries, and these movements seem cyclical, as Figure 1–1 shows. With less regularity, a cyclical pattern also prevails in Asia and the Middle East, though it is interesting to note that the latter region offers the greatest resistance to the development of assemblies, both in its traditional monarchies and in its "progressive" republics (Iraq or Syria). These cyclical movements show the weaknesses of assemblies and their shaky basis, but they also show the strength of their support.

Moreover, in Western countries, in Communist countries, and in a somewhat less clear-cut fashion in the Third World, the rubber-stamp character of legislatures may not be as widespread and uniform as has been suggested by some commentators. Possibly because critics in Western countries have complained about the small influence of many legislatures, a renewed interest in the activities of legislators has come to indicate that it is feasible, though within somewhat narrow limits, for legislatures to act with independence and effectiveness. In some of the Communist states, including the Soviet Union, the legislature has been somewhat more involved in national affairs since the 1950s. More detailed analyses, though still quite limited, have shown that there were variations among Third World legislatures and that their role may be on the increase, often with the encouragement of the executive.

THE FUNCTIONS OF LEGISLATURES

2

What are the functions of legislatures? Almost everywhere, they seem less influential than they were expected to be, although they have survived in a large majority of countries. Should one blame executives for their demise, or should one not rather go back to the functions of legislatures and ask whether the functions they can perform are somewhat different, and perhaps less exalted, than those which were given to them? Legislatures were created primarily to deliberate on the laws and to pass them. Could it be that they are not really equipped to be the main agents of the lawmaking process?

THE FAILINGS OF THE ORIGINAL BLUEPRINT OF THE LEGISLATURES' ROLE In Chapter 1 we saw that the difficulty of the analysis of legislatures stemmed in large part from a misconception about the nature of lawmaking which led in turn to a misconception about the part which legislatures could be called upon to play in the legislative and policy-making processes. This misunderstanding arose principally for two reasons. First, "laws" or "statutes" are not, or are no longer, what they were supposed to be. Laws were supposed to cover general questions and important questions, but it is not possible to define "generality" and "importance." In practice, there is continuous progression from unimportant to important matters, with no point at which a break can be found. It is one of the failings of legal thinking that it tends to dichotomize or at least to divide sharply between areas where no sharp distinction exists. A matter is legally dealt with by statute or it is not, but it cannot be labeled "important" or "unimportant" in the same dichotomous fashion.

Yet this is perhaps not the major failing of the theory. The major problem arises from the fact that legal distinctions tend to be static. A matter is dealt with by a statute *today*, but if conditions are changed tomorrow, the statute will still remain valid. And situations do change continuously. As a result, statutes are always, to a greater or lesser degree, behind the reality. If we look at any field in which government acts, whether economic growth, educational development, or welfare services, we see continuous changes. But statutes can only deal with these matters incrementally, changing in periodic jumps in a vain effort to keep up. This is what distinguishes "statutes" from "policies," for policies are dynamic—they adapt to situations, whereas statutes remain the same until they are changed, and changing a statute is a difficult and usually slow process.

If legislatures are essentially involved in lawmaking, therefore, they are also necessarily hampered with respect to policies. Why is it, however, that this state of affairs, which seems so loaded against the legislature, was so completely overlooked by the classical theorists who drew up the blueprints for representative assemblies? The answer is simple. When theorists began thinking about legislatures, they faced a situation which was wholly different from the one that confronts most modern governments. Locke and Montesquieu looked at societies in which state involvement in social and economic matters was minimal if not nonexistent. For them, statutes not did mean education or housing acts; they covered problems of private property, individual rights, family law—in short the regulation of private relationships between individuals. Slowly the balance tilted, through the nineteenth and twentieth centuries, toward public legislation establishing new agencies and regulating social and economic matters. But no one drew the conclusion that this entailed a different type of involvement for legislatures. Indeed, this conclusion easily could have been drawn from the examination of the classics themselves, for Locke had isolated foreign affairs from the field of legislative activity precisely because matters were held to be urgent and continuous in the field of foreign affairs.[1] With the involvement of the state in social and economic matters now also often urgent and always continuous, the same considerations would seem to apply to legislative involvement in domestic affairs. It would have been much more fruitful to explore the role to be given to legislatures in foreign affairs than to attempt to consider social and economic policy as a subset of private law; if, instead of concentrating on lawmaking of a traditional (private individual) kind, the analysis of legislative involvement had taken into account what legislation and policy-making had increasingly become, some of the difficulties relating to the role of legislatures might have been seen in a somewhat different light.

[1] John Locke, *Second Treatise on Civil Government*, Chapter XII.

TOWARDS A
DETERMINATION OF
THE FUNCTIONS
OF LEGISLATURES

THE BASIC COMPONENTS OF THE MODEL:
INFLUENCE AND PARTICIPATION IN A PROCESS OF CHANGE

Let us move away from the dichotomy between "general" and "particular" and consider the real question which arises, that of the quantity of change over a whole variety of issues, some of which have a limited impact—for instance, because they affect few people—and some of which have a much larger impact. The influence of the legislature is obviously measured by the extent to which it contributes to this change, or, negatively, by the extent to which it prevents change from taking place.

Two important consequences follow from such an approach. First, the problem has to be viewed in an incremental fashion. We may talk loosely about "radical" or "profound" transformations, but the reality is always that some changes of a given magnitude occur in certain fields. Consequently, if we introduce a legislature in a country, it can modify only by a finite amount a situation which it has to take as given. The notion of *tabula rasa,* or even of a "fresh start," is clearly a myth, although it can more easily be upheld in matters of private law, if only at the price of neglecting sociological and psychological realities. A legislature is relatively free to modify private relationships, whereas on matters such as economic growth, educational development, and social welfare, the "supremacy" of legislatures is limited by realities to minor adjustments. However powerful the Haitian legislature may be, it cannot in one year decide that the per capital income of Haiti will equal that of the United States, but it could decide to adopt French, British, or Soviet divorce laws. Legislative insertion in the life of a given country, therefore, must be based on a dynamic view of change constrained by the realities of the present.

The second consequence is that the distinction between "general" and particular becomes a choice of the decision-makers within the overall process of change. Traditional legislative theory suggests that the legislature is concerned with general matters because such matters are the only ones which count; if and when the balance sheet of all decisions of a government is produced, detailed matters will be given a much smaller weighting than general matters, but the number of general changes may be so small that the benefits gained from detailed changes are comparatively large. Moreover, there is a constant two-way relationship between general and detailed matters: changes of a detailed character during a period may pave the way toward more general changes subsequently.

We should, therefore, analyze the legislative process and the involvement of legislatures on a broad front which embraces detailed questions as well as general matters within the context of a changing society or of one that resists change. Such an analysis implies that the "classical" model of legislative activity must be replaced with one which takes into account the role of individual legislators. However free the system, legislators operate under some constraints—they will do so much and not more over each problem that comes up and, therefore, over the whole range of issues they will not be prepared to extend the involvement of the legislature beyond a given specific point which can be calculated. The executive has a large part to play in the determination of this point, for its influence is one of the constraints; but as legislators go at least to the point which the executive allows, they do participate, however infrequently, in the total decision process.

It therefore follows that the tradeoff problem between broad or general questions and more detailed questions has in reality to be seen not only in terms of the overall change effected at the broad level compared to the sum of the detailed changes, but also in terms of the legislator's sense of the efficacy of legislation on detailed matters compared to his sense of the efficacy of legislation on general matters. He is likely to think that the amount of resources he will have to spend in order to bring about a broad change will be such that his efficacy will be low, whereas he is much more likely to be able to effect some change, however minute, at the detailed level. Hence there is an underlying propensity for legislatures to be concerned with detailed matters, and not, as the "classics" would have had it, a propensity to go to generalities. From this one can also see that the behavior which was decried by Lowell and Bryce as being almost "unworthy" of legislatures because it was strictly much too detailed and sectional is indeed quite normal.

In this assessment of the involvement of legislatures in the affairs of a nation, the problem is thus one of adequately measuring involvement which manifests itself through limited and incremental actions at a whole variety of levels. That is to say, we neither can expect all power for the legislature in any field (whatever its legal powers may be) nor should we exclude the possibility of legislative intervention in any field. Intervention by the legislature takes the form of influence and participation; there is no clear dichotomy between decision and nondecision. A whole variety of points of penetration of the legislature exists in the political system and they help to define a series of functions, in regard to each of which legislators are both responsible and responsible only in part.

We can now apply these components of the involvement of legislatures to legislative activities and determine the functions of legislatures.

In relation to the demand-making part of the political system, legislatures may serve as intermediaries for demands made by others or may themselves serve as originators of suggestions. The functions of legislatures in this respect vary, therefore, between the two extreme poles of sheer communication or transmission and initiation, with an infinite number of intermediate positions inasmuch as the legislature or legislator may modify the suggestion which has been made, may aggregate this suggestion, with others, or may perform any of a number of other operations. These suggestions may be pitched at various degrees of generality, ranging from simply the demand of a constitutent for an increase of compensation for some damage on his property to the presentation of a complete economic policy designed to change the level of development of the country. At the demand level, detailed pressures are likely to come from individual legislators, partly from their own ideas and partly to channel the views of constitutents and pressure groups, whereas general pressure is likely to arise if some degree of agreement can be obtained between legislators. General pressures therefore, are likely to emanate from groups of legislators such as committees.

In relation to outputs of the political system, activities also will range from very detailed to very general; they either will result from the initiatives of members or will be triggered by constituents and interests. Individual legislators will be more concerned, and potentially more successful, where the output is of a detailed kind; where the output is more general (as in policy statements or bills), legislators will have to combine and outputs of one period will generate demands for the next and a prior unsuccessful attempt will lead to further action.

It also follows that the degree of involvement and influence of legislatures depends necessarily on a variety of constraints. These may be "narrow" if the legislators are afraid to question the executive, the leadership of the party, or the military. Social and economic constraints also will limit the scope of activity of legislatures in that, given other priorities and only moderate information, alternative courses of action are often precluded. The overall influence of a legislature has to be assessed over time, the functions of the legislature being essentially measured through its ability to adopt and pass on, on the one hand, and to initiate, on the other, a whole variety of reactions to existing situations and to previous policies. The more detailed these situations and policies, the more the action can be measured over a short period; the more the situations and policies are general, the more the involvement needs to be measured over a long period.

When examined in this way, the functions of legislatures cover a much greater span than the classical theory was prepared to allow. These activities are all equally justified, so that the role of legislators legitimately extends much beyond a concern with general matters. This makes it possible to subsume in a single model the somewhat divided list of roles which are sometimes ascribed to legislatures in the contemporary literature. When it is suggested that legislative systems manage conflict and integrate the policy, it is simply stated that these systems participate in decision-making at a whole variety of levels. When it is suggested that the means by which conflict management is achieved is through deliberation, decision, adjudication, and catharsis, this is merely a list of the types of activities by which legislators can achieve success in conflict management. To say that authorizations, legitimization, and representation are part of integration is also merely to specify that ideas come to be channeled outputs or come to be approved, positively or by tacit agreement, by the legislature.[2] The legislative process is ubiquitous at any given moment and its effects have to be seen over time.

LEGISLATIVE INSTRUMENTS OR TECHNIQUES OF ACTION

For legislatures to be effective at detailed as well as at general levels, instruments or procedures appropriate to each level have to exist. A specific suggestion concerning one constituent cannot be handled in the same way as a general problem. Yet, because legislatures have been created in order to pass statutes, the procedures available to them are often in fact not very appropriate. What we see is a curious situation in which legislatures have become the prisoners of the procedures invented in the past, necessitating efforts to distort these procedures from their original purpose. The procedure of lawmaking has become an instrument by which legislators have tended to meet such problems as (1) helping individual constituents; (2) raising issues in order to obtain an administrative change; (3) proposing long-term policy alterations on which the government, fellow legislators, and the public at large have to be made aware of a problem. When a legislator proposes a bill to a committee, he may know very well that the bill will not pass, but he simply uses the procedure which he has at his disposal to air the issue.

Let us try to be a little more precise about the nature of the problem. On the one hand, legislatures have a variety of functions, ranging from general to particular; these cover both the inputs and the outputs of the

---

[2] See in particular M. E. Jewell and S. C. Patterson, *The Legislative Process in the United States* (New York: Random House, Inc., 1966), Chapter I, pp. 5–25, for a description of these legislative functions.

political system. In practice, this may mean, on the input side (1) putting pressure for a very narrow question—for instance, the naturalization of a foreigner; (2) suggesting changes of an intermediate character in the context of a broader problem—for instance, modifying laws on drunken driving; (3) proposing a major change—for instance, proposing a state pension scheme. On the output side, this may mean (1) trying to stop or modify an administrative decision—for instance, the decision to locate a state agency office in a particular building; (2) wanting to modify regulations or clauses of proposed government bills; (3) wanting to oppose a major governmental policy or a major government bill. One can see that, in these last two aspects, reactions to outputs may cover opposing either governmental policy decisions (e.g., by regulations or, as in foreign affairs or economic policy, by other types of executive decisions) or proposed legislation. Yet the purpose of the activity of the legislator is similar, whether the matter is dealt with by regulation or by statute.

How can the legislators achieve these various goals? They are constrained by procedures and therefore are in large part constrained by what the constitution says about their powers and by what custom has added to the constitution. Constitutions naturally have emphasised lawmaking. As a result, each of the goals which the legislator has in mind will have to be pressed for through the means of the constitutionally or customarily established procedures for lawmaking. In order to achieve what they wish, legislators are led to use bills and amendments as tricks. This is particularly done in the field of financial legislation, where, in order to discuss a particular administrative problem or even some general policy, legislators often propose to cut or amend in a minor fashion the estimates of a government agency. This is also why bills are presented, as they allow for debates which make it possible to air a question.

One can complain about the fact that tricks are used in this way, yet for many problems there are no other means at the disposal of legislators. Legislators have, however, developed new procedures. These are still limited and tend to be found more frequently in older legislatures. The problem with them is that they are often relatively ineffective because of their informality. One such procedure is the debate which can be used to discuss both broad matters and limited problems. The question is a type of small debate, which has taken roots mainly in the United Kingdom and, with variations, in the Commonwealth. Another type of development is the committee structure. Committees were originally lawmaking bodies, and to a large extent this is what they remain. They help the legislatures to deliberate on bills, but they also have taken on the function of inquiry, initially to investigate bills, and increasingly irrespective of bills. As a result—mainly in the United States—legislative committees have taken on a scrutiny function; in the United Kingdom and elsewhere specially constituted committees are in-

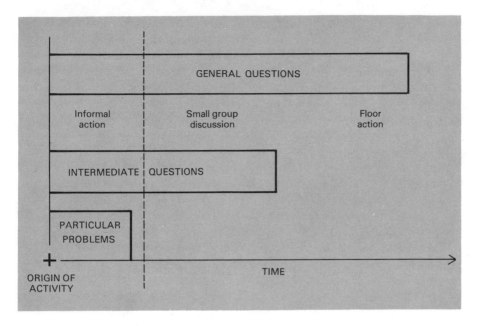

Figure 2–1   Time, informality of discussion, and extent of generality of the problem.

volved in administrative scrutiny. Finally, there are more informal means, ③ which range from the face-to-face discussion with ministers and officials to letters and written questions. These usually are not connected to the legislative process and have developed independently, mainly as a natural result of the fact that legislators knew ministers and civil servants and executives found it politically useful to appear to be helpful.

These various procedures enable legislators to be a little better adapted to the functions which they have to fulfill. Some of these more informal procedures are of critical importance for some types of inputs and some types of output control. But it must always be remembered that these new procedures remain subsidiary, that lawmaking is the procedure *par excellence*, and that new legislatures are unlikely to develop them rapidly. Moreover, even if the instruments which legislatures use do enable members to perform a variety of functions, this is often at the cost of using these instruments beyond their original aims and at the cost of spending resources in an inefficient fashion. Lawmaking is a wasteful activity in many of its aspects because it is distorted from its original aims. Used as it has often been to meet the legal structures that require a chamber to use debate in order to air a problem, it contributes in part to the disrepute of some legislatures because the law is not passed in the end or because only few members are involved in the question. Being the most overt and well-known part of the activities of assemblies, it tends to be the subject of much criticism and the occasion for little credit, particularly as it contributes to seeing problems on a much more detailed and instantaneous fashion than should realistically be the case. The less publicized activities of assemblies, which are informal and even sometimes concealed, often deserve more examination and may lead to more influence. But they are, after all, less well known, and the difficulty of knowing them in detail has hampered to a very large extent the study of legislatures. We need, therefore, to consider the problems of access and knowledge before we embark on the study of the influence of legislatures in the contemporary world.

THE METHODOLOGICAL DIFFICULTIES OF THE STUDY OF LEGISLATURES

3

Despite their importance in the theory of representative government, legislatures have been little studied, at least on a comparative basis. Numerous works exist on parties and the military, but in the field of legislatures there has as yet been very little which can genuinely be recognized as comparative. Indeed, only very recently have works been written which, in their successive studies of a number of legislatures, even begin to compare with the early studies of Bryce and especially Lowell, who in fact gives a description of legislative behavior at the end of the nineteenth century in Europe which is much more precise than anything to be found in most of the recent work.[1]

One reason for this lack of work probably has been, for a period at least, lack of interest. The spread of "behavioral" approaches to comparative government has meant that political scientists have been more drawn toward the study of interest groups and parties, as well as of the bureaucracy and the military, than of "constitutional bodies," of which legislatures are perhaps the most clear-cut example. This lack of interest resulted in large part from the apparent demise of legislatures in many countries: if an assembly is a mere rubber stamp, why should political scientists bother to study it?

Yet this is only part of the reason, for political scientists hitherto have not sufficiently bothered to find out whether, indeed, assemblies are rubber stamps or something a bit more active. The fact that the Supreme Soviet of

[1] See the bibliography at the end of this book for contemporary work on legislatures. But, apart from the legislatures of some of the major Western countries, studies have been very scanty on the subject up to very recently.

the Soviet Union is held to be a rubber stamp is no justification for not studying the Korean or Venezuelan legislature. Moreover, even those legislatures which have been studied—indeed, perhaps overstudied—are still profoundly unknown from the most important standpoint, namely that of their effective overall influence. The American Congress has given rise to a very large number of studies ranging from the most general and all-embracing to detailed case studies of either some particular structures (*The House Rules Committee*, for instance [2]) or of the passage of some bills (e.g. *Congress makes a law* [3]). Yet no study of the United States House or Senate measures comprehensively the overall influence of Congress over a wide variety of fields, and therefore attempts to build a general theory of the types of influence and of roles of congressmen are nonexistent. Most studies include a surprising amount of purely juridical description of the rules of the various bodies, and much attention has been devoted to the attitudes of congressmen (although, with the exception of roll call studies, the best-known studies in this field refer to legislators in the individual states and not in the Congress).[4] But except for case studies, which by definition can give only insights and cannot provide a basis for generalizations, there is surprisingly little on the real influence of Congress and congressmen. And this is *a fortiori* true of other legislatures, where, as with the British, French, and other European parliaments, most of the work has consisted in obtaining a broad panorama of overall activities and in describing, mainly in historical terms, the role of these legislatures over a few issues.

Thus, although one of the reasons for the absence of comparative studies has been a lack of interest in these bodies and *a priori* views about their lack of importance, the full explanation has to come from other causes as well. These are to be found in the severe methodological problems which the study of legislatures raises and which can be expected to be solved only very slowly and may indeed never be completely overcome.

DATA GATHERING IN THE FIELD OF LEGISLATIVE ANALYSIS

At least three aspects of data gathering in the field of legislature studies constitute severe handicaps. First, published or publishable documents are often difficult to obtain. No legislature is entirely free from blame in this respect, as some activities always remain unrecorded; where committee hearings, for

---

[2] J. A. Robinson, *The House Rules Committee* (Indianapolis: The Bobbs-Merrill Co., 1963).

[3] S. K. Bailey, *Congress makes a law* (the 1946 Employment Act) (New York: Columbia University Press, 1950).

[4] See Chapter 7.

instance, are published, the full debates of the proceedings themselves might well not be published; proceedings of subcommittees, which can be of importance, may not be published at all, even where those of the main committees can be found in their entirety.

These problems face those studying the United States legislature, and, to a greater extent, the legislatures of other Western countries, and problems of data gathering are appreciably larger if one attempts to study non-Western legislatures. For a variety of reasons, among which the deliberate desire to conceal the proceedings of these assemblies is only one, it is extremely difficult to obtain complete records of even the plenary sessions of many legislatures. Some countries do not print these proceedings verbatim; voting figures often are not given; committee memberships, texts of resolutions or questions, and other ancillary documents are not always published.

Secondly, we have little information about informal activities, which, by their very nature, tend to go unrecorded. As a result, information has to be collected in a roundabout fashion and in particular through surveys of legislators. This method, unfortunately, has limitations, and is slow and costly.[5] We have, therefore, a very patchy knowledge of the involvement of legislators in various aspects of their public life and even less knowledge of their informal activities. Indeed, we have to be reconciled to the fact that some informal activities simply cannot be known—in some countries because members fear to talk, and in all countries simply because the most informal activities are not revealed at the time. Legislators are engaged in operations of manipulation of their colleagues and other leading public figures which they would not wish to mention as long as they take place. Narrations of past events are an unsatisfactory substitute because memories fade away and activities become idealized. What we can hope to obtain about informal activities will always be incomplete at best.

As long as surveys of informal activities are not undertaken on a broad scale, however, we have to be content with even less. Our knowledge of activities in a legislature being mainly restricted to the formal portion, inferences have to be made about more informal aspects. Although many behind-the-scenes actions have real impact, we have to be content with those which reach a "critical mass" and leave some traces. These will be only the ones which have an impact on future activities and on the country's

[5] See Chapter 7, pp. 76–91.

policies, and they constitute only a very small part of those that have been left by the wayside and about which we shall remain, in almost all cases, totally ignorant.

THE PROBLEMS OF COMPARISON: THE DETERMINATION OF FUNCTIONAL EQUIVALENTS

When we examined the functions and the techniques by which functions are performed in Chapter 2, we encountered another type of methodological problem: the same procedures may perform different functions. Question time may constitute a means of pressure in one legislature, in another a way for legislators to introduce a bill. If we are to compare two countries only, we may be able to cope with this difficulty, but, on a broader cross-national basis, the problem may appear insuperable. It may have been one of the reasons why most studies have remained nation-bound or have at best considered a small number of countries. We have to devise functional equivalents for each of the legislatures under study, and this task is vast if we want to go further than the vague statement that a given technique in one legislature corresponds "in part" to another technique in another chamber. Indeed, our task will be no less than the reconstruction of the whole of the activities of the legislature on the basis of the different functions performed. If it so happens—and we can predict that this will be the case—that the object and characteristics of laws which are discussed in one legislature differ from those of another, only by undertaking a precise "reconstruction" of legislative activities in terms of functions performed shall we be able to compare adequately the two legislatures. There are other procedures, moreover, such as written questions, "adjournment motions," debates over the appointment of individuals, and so forth, which are even more difficult to classify and to reassign to various functions. Such an operation is not theoretically impossible, but it is long and complex and the success it meets depends on the amount of knowledge which we have on each legislature.

Given that few legislatures have been studied, even superficially, let alone in depth, we cannot expect the idea of "functional equivalents" to be used more than in a general and imprecise fashion, at least at present. All we can do is draw attention to the problem, so that we remember that, by using a given technique in a given way, a given legislature tends to perform a function more fully than another legislature which uses primarily other techniques to fulfill the same function.

THE MEASUREMENT OF THE ROLE OF LEGISLATURES: PARTICIPATION IN DECISION-MAKING AND THE EXAMINATION OF INFLUENCE OVER TIME

Of all the methodogical difficulties which beset the study of legislatures, perhaps the largest concerns the analysis of the relationship between these bodies and their environment. The study of legislatures is not, *by itself,* interesting. It is interesting only if we can throw some light on the question of the influence of legislatures on the political process and on the ways in which this influence is exercised. What difference does it make if a country has a legislature and what is the direction of that difference are the main questions. Yet we can answer these questions only if we can measure influence within the political process. We noted earlier that the all-or-nothing attitude stemming from the concentration of the role of legislatures on lawmaking led to an underestimate of the part played by legislatures in the political process as a whole. By substituting a theory of influence for the original dichotomy of laws and executive decisions, it becomes possible to see legislatures intervening in a variety of ways over many problems; but the study of influence in other fields is not very advanced and the various studies which have been undertaken, in the field of community power in particular, have given only few insights into the general problem, while raising large numbers of methodological and substantive controversies.[6]

 There are two important ways in which the study of influence in the legislative area can take place; both will help to bring about a better understanding of the overall influence problem. One is the question of *importance* in relation to a variety of activities of politicians and political bodies. This can be studied by considering the whole of the policies pursued by public bodies in a given political unit (for instance a national unit) and by using a number of indicators, such as the number of people involved or, more precisely, the intensity with which sections of the population are involved in the problem, the money spent and other resources employed, or the extent of popular "feeling" and thus the psychological costs of introducing the change.[7] Some indicators are easier to operationalize than others; the

---

[6] See N. W. Polsby, *Community Power and Political Theory* (New Haven: Yale University Press, 1963).

[7] See T. J. Lowi, "American business, Public policies and Political Theory," *World Politics*, July 1964, pp. 677–715; R. H. Salisbury, "The analysis of Public Policy: a search for Theories and Roles," in A. Ranney, *Political Science and Public Policy* (Chicago: Markham, 1968), p. 158; J. Blondel et al., "Legislative behaviour: some steps towards a cross-national measurement," *Government and Opposition*, Winter 1969, pp. 73–74.

data at our disposal may be very scanty for many countries and many periods for some indicators. But they can be used. One thus can assess the extent to which the legislature has become involved in the policies of the country. If we find that an economic plan, for instance, does not involve the legislature at all, or if we find, conversely, that the legislature spends most of its time on matters of private law while social and economic policies are decided outside it, the importance of the legislative body begins to appear. We also can begin to see what seem to be the minimum and maximum limits, in the real world, of the involvement of legislatures. In this way we can embark on an empirical theory of what this influence is. Such involvement, of course, should not be restricted to the lawmaking process but should cover all the ways in which a legislature is involved.

The second step to follow involves measuring the involvement of legislatures over time. Even for the best studied legislatures, such as the United States Congress, work has tended to be done on the basis of an instantaneous examination of the results of legislative action. Students of legislatures have worked as if personal or collective influence was bound to leave its mark on all but a few months. Of course, this approach is encouraged by the techniques of action of legislatures for each bill can be seen on its own: a bill is passed or not, and executive-legislative relations are measured by this one criterion. If one wishes to refine the study, one may examine committee procedure, consider amendments, and state rather more precisely how much of the original bill remains at the final stage, but this is still deducing influence from very short-term actions.

In fact, as we had occasion to note in Chapter 2, only in a preliminary examination is it possible to suggest that bills are "one-shot" affairs; the socialization process which goes on before, through, and after the bill suggests that it is only one bead which needs to be seen alongside many others if it is to be assessed in a comprehensive way. "Scores" based on successes or failures, in the field of lawmaking, are thus necessarily very misleading, if not wholly misleading: if, as may well be the case, the same type of bill, relating to the same idea, is presented each year over a ten-year period, and if the bill eventually comes through only at the end, it is not as interesting to note the defeat of nine bills as to note that it took ten years for the suggestion to go through, either because the executive had its way in the end or because backbenchers slowly convinced the government. Thus, if one tries to measure the relative strengths of United States Presidents and Congresses by examining, on a year-by-year-basis, what percentage of important laws stemming from presidential initiative passed in the Congress, one is not only bound to give higher scores to Presidents who did nothing than to Presidents who did much, but one is also bound to underestimate the strength of a President who, aware of the time it takes to socialize an assembly, feels that his best strategy is to present fairly similar bills, if not the same bill, at a number of sessions.

The decision-making process, therefore, must be seen as one which, over a period of years, leads to a number of changes in a variety of areas. Legislatures and individual legislators exercise their influence, even if slowly, within this ongoing process. Questions presented in a legislature at one point in time may trigger further questions in a subsequent period; these in turn may lead to bills being discussed and, where the government is "strong" but responsive, to the executive itself presenting a bill in the course of a future session. Such an approach will indeed help toward the development of a theory of "functional equivalents" which will show the ways in which legislators use different techniques in the various stages of the socialization and decision process. What is more, studying influence over time also will enable political scientists to discover how long it takes for problems to be raised and settled in different fields. It will then become possible to distinguish between various types of fields in terms of real sensitivity; and by leading to comparisons between legislatures over these different fields, this technique will make it possible to know more about the relative time span of ideas and the apparent duration of the "socialization process" in various legislatures and various polities.

Although the need for them is clear, studies over time have scarcely been undertaken. As a result, in this book much of what we shall say about legislatures will remain imprecise, because the difficulties which we outlined, ranging from data gathering to the measurement of influence, limit the testing of hypotheses and, indeed, the scope of inquiries. But the study of legislative behavior is increasingly coming nearer to the goal of the analysis of influence and the methodological difficulties are being circumscribed. The analysis of activities of legislatures on a cross-national basis, therefore, will produce increasingly large payoffs in the field of the theory of influence in general as well as in the field of legislative influence in particular.

THE CONSTITUTIONAL FRAMEWORK OF POWERS

4

Although we must expect that the real influence of legislators will be at variance with their constitutional powers, we nevertheless need to know what scope constitutions give to legislatures before we can consider some of the more complex problems of legislative influence. For a large number of countries, admittedly, the legislature has a symbolic character and is a corollary and a manifestation of support for the principle of popular sovereignty. But the extent to which countries vary in the lip service which they pay to assembly importance is interesting in itself.

These variations are large. Firstly, there are variations on the principle of assembly sovereignty itself. Some countries limit the powers of the assembly directly; others do so through the use of the referendum. Secondly, more detailed limitations have been introduced on ideological or on technical grounds, ostensibly in order to enable the machinery of government to work smoothly and to stop undue legislative encroachments. The development of legislatures and of executive-legislative relations in the last two centuries has led to an expertise which can appropriately be described as a form of "constitutional engineering." By looking at all the constitutional arrangements which exist in the contemporary world, we can have a clearer idea of the current situation on a number of important points.[1] Theorists suggest that assemblies should be sovereign, but is this in fact what constitutions say they are? And if constitutions introduce limitations, what kinds of limitations are these? Even if such a study does not reveal much about real influence, it does reveal the state of the prevailing ideologies across the world on what assemblies should be like.

[1] See Appendix I.

**THE SYMBOLIC
AUTHORITY OF
LEGISLATURES**

Naturally enough, the first question to look at is that of the overall status or "authority" which constitutions give to assemblies. If representative government is upheld in a country, the assembly is likely to be recognized as sovereign, at least in the field of lawmaking and within the constitution. Thus the assembly will have at least symbolic importance, and this symbolic importance is certainly enhanced by the fact that very few countries do not elect their legislature by universal suffrage of both sexes. Indeed, since Switzerland introduced votes for women at the federal level in 1971, only a few Middle Eastern countries have held out for an all-male electorate. Very few countries impose literacy requirements; those that do are mainly located in Latin America, and even there the requirements are gradually disappearing. In Europe, only Portugal and Spain impose limitations, and in the rest of the world South Africa and Rhodesia are the two main exceptions to the general rule of universal suffrage. There may be various forms of limitations and harassments in practice, for electoral systems are subject to marked variations and manipulations.[2] But these inequalities exist despite the principle of universal suffrage, though they may not always be juridically unconstitutional.

Let us look at the extent to which democratically elected legislatures are accorded a high symbolic status. Four indicators of such a symbolic status can be found: (1) parliamentary immunity (the right to make statements in the House); (2) parliamentary inviolability (the right not to be detained except in certain circumstances); (3) procedural independence (the right to draft freely the rules of the chamber); and (4) freedom of meeting (the right to meet whenever members so decide). All four rights are given widely, though there are variations and interesting "silences" in a number of countries. The majority of constitutions give their legislators full parliamentary immunity (69 countries, or almost two-thirds of the universe); a slightly larger number (76, or nearly three-quarters) give some form of inviolability from arrest, but only three constitutions give full inviolability— this may be considered, however, to be going further than necessary, since it means that no arrest at all, even of people caught in the act, can be made. The power given to the assembly to establish its own rules of procedure is the right which is most widely given by constitutions to legislatures (82 countries, or exactly three-quarters), while the freedom of assembly is much more restricted in relation to sessions: a large majority of constitutions restrict the periods of meetings of legislatures to sessions specified in the constitution (84 countries) and only in half the polities with assemblies (54)

---

[2] See W. J. Mackenzie, *Free Elections* (London: George Allen & Unwin, 1958).

is it possible for the legislature to decide on its own about extraordinary sessions. Indeed, the number of countries in which the assembly is free to close such extraordinary sessions when it wishes is even smaller (29, or less than a third).

Variations with respect to these symbolic rights seem to be spread to some extent at random. However, in Communist countries the symbolic status of legislatures is particularly high. Differences elsewhere are often tied to whether the country is a monarchy or not, for even in those monarchies where the king has ceased to play any significant part in the conduct of governmental affairs, the meetings of the legislature often are opened and closed at will by the king (in effect, of course, by the executive), while this right is granted less commonly and with more restrictions to the executive in a Republic. The status of a legislature depends, therefore, in part on whether a country has had a history of unbroken constitutional development.

SECOND CHAMBERS

The debate for or against second chambers has a very long history. Second chambers usually have been frowned upon by democrats on the grounds that they limit the sovereignty of the people. It is therefore interesting to note that, nonetheless, almost half the countries of the world have second chambers (in 1971, 52 countries out of 108; Yugoslavia in fact has five chambers). What is more, the decline in the number of countries with bicameral arrangements is very slow, being particularly marked in Atlantic countries (Sweden being the most recent case but practically imperceptible elsewhere.[3] Very few African states have second chambers, but a majority of states in the Atlantic and Latin American areas, which contain the oldest polities, have them. They exist more frequently among Commonwealth countries than in the rest of the Third World and the Communist world. They tend to exist in older and more traditional countries (Afghanistan or Ethiopia) or where the polity, though not having been independent for a long period, has had a cultural identity. They are more widespread in large states than in small countries and, as could be expected, in federal rather than unitary states.

Thus the age of the country, its size, and its unified character have a part to play in the existence of second chambers, irrespective of the "ideology" of the political system. For this reason it becomes interesting to

[3] Since World War II, the second chamber was abolished in New Zealand, Denmark, Haiti, Kenya and Sweden; a second chamber was created in Turkey, Paraguay, Ghana, and Czechoslovakia.

look at the matter more closely and to see whether the composition and powers of second chambers account for their relatively widespread appearances. Yet it appears that they are rarely elected proportionately to the population (this is so only in about 10 countries) and that their constitutional status is often equal to that of the first chamber (22 cases). Second chambers, therefore, are not about to disappear, nor are they about to relinquish their position, nor are they likely to be made to reflect the composition of the country on a democratic basis.

A *priori*, it seems that second chambers should be strong in three types of circumstances: first, when the composition of the chamber is very undemocratic and the regime is traditional; second, when the composition of the chamber is democratic and the justification for the second chamber is precisely the democratic basis of its composition; and third, in federal countries. When powers and composition are considered together, however, the reality can be seen to be quite different, although there is some validity in the last two of the three hypotheses just enumerated. First, and perhaps most surprisingly, it is not true that second chambers are used to buttress traditional regimes. Second, second chambers are somewhat stronger in federal states than in other countries, but not overwhelmingly so. Third, the hypothesis which is best validated is that which suggests that second chambers will be stronger where their composition is democratic. If second chambers are divided into "strong" and "weak" on the basis of whether they have or have not powers equal to those of the first chamber in lawmaking powers, and if they are divided according to whether the basis of selection is proportional to the whole population, whether some advantage is given to smaller regions, whether there is equality of regions or provinces, and whether appointment is by the head of state without election, the breakdown is that shown in Table 4–1. (Yugoslavia is excluded as there are five chambers in that country.)

Thus second chambers tend on the whole to be weaker where members are appointed and stronger where apportionment is proportional to the population. But they are also stronger where regions are given an equal

Table 4-1. Selection and Powers of Second Chambers

	Proportional	Regional Advantage	Regional Equality	Appointment without Election
Strong	9	2	9	2
Weak	3	12	4	8
Impossible to assess			1	1
Total	12	14	14	11

number of members (for instances, the United States Senate), which is indeed a greater distortion than when they are elected on the basis of *some* advantage given to particular regions (for instance, when rural areas are favored, as in France).

It might be thought that the explanation for this variation can be traced simply to the existence of federal states: as is well known, some federal states, such as the United States, Australia or Switzerland, give the same number of representatives to each state or province in the second chamber, the logic being that these regions should be represented as semi-sovereign states. It is of course also well known that this principle does not apply to all federal states, of the fifteen federal states which had legislatures in 1971 (Nigeria and Argentina were under military rule), only one did not have a second chamber (Cameroon), and another, Yugoslavia, had five chambers and cannot easily be compared. Of the remaining thirteen states, about half apportioned their second chamber on the basis of equality of representation of the component units, but only two of these have "weak" second chambers. The other half allowed for some distortion short of equality (West Germany, the USSR, and Canada in particular); in four of these cases, the second chamber was "weak."

Three conclusions emerge: the first is that "weak" second chambers exist in federal states as well as in unitary states; the second is that in federal states, second chambers selected on the basis of an equal number of members per region are stronger than those where the basis of selection establishes a *smaller* distortion; but the third is that the same trend exists also in unitary states, as can be seen from Table 4–2, which refers only to unitary states.

Thus federalism neither accounts for the principle of equality between provinces as a basis for the selection of the second chamber nor for the fact that the constitutions of these polities tend to give the same powers to both chambers. What seems to be operating is, therefore, a somewhat different principle, possibly derived originally from federalism—and indeed from imitation of the United States, for the cases of "equality" include Chile,

Table 4-2. Selection and Powers of Second Chambers in Unitary States

	Proportional	Regional Advantage	Regional Equality	Appointment without Election
Strong	9	1	3	2
Weak	3	8	2	8
Impossible to assess			1	1
Total	12	9	6	11

Ecuador, and Liberia.[4] Nevertheless, federalism also can lead to forms other than complete equality between the regions, but in this situation federal second chambers are as weak as second chambers of unitary states. On the other hand, when there is equality of representation of component units, second chambers are generally strong, whether the country is federal or not. Equality of representation of regions is thus a legitimacy principle for second chambers alongside the proportional representation of the population.

In about half the countries, first chambers are the embodiment of the "popular will." In the other half, there is also a second chamber, and this chamber is usually given strong powers either if it, too, embodies the popular will on some basis not altogether different from that of the first chamber or if it gives equal representation to each of the territorial components of the nation. This confirms the tendency for constitutions of the contemporary world to embody the democratic principle through the election of the legislature, while adding a limitation; it also suggests that perhaps the long-standing argument over second chambers has lost much of its ideological reality.

THE CURBS ON THE DECISION-MAKING POWERS OF LEGISLATURES

Even if legitimized by popular election, legislatures may be curbed by the constitution. Such curbs may be based on three types of justifications, which can be labeled the democratic justification, the oligarchical justification and the technical-practical justification. The democratic or participationist justification for restrictions stems from the idea that representative government is insufficient to translate the popular will into politics. Some form of "direct appeal to the people," therefore, will be introduced and this will justify the reduction of the legislature's constitutional powers. It is interesting to examine a little more closely the nature of this claim as it has taken, almost from the moment when legislatures were created, two sharply distinct forms. One is the straight participationist line, according to which the people are allowed to intervene directly in the making of laws through referendums. The Swiss constitution is, of course, the most extreme case of the application of the principle, but popular involvement soon also took the form of personal, charismatic, or plebiscitary support given to a leader. Support for the legislature can thus be counterbalanced by support for a man. The presidential system on the United States model is one of the mildest forms of such a constitutional approach, with the legislature being granted many powers, though not that of making and

---

[4] In 1971 the Socialist President of Chile began moving toward a constitutional change which would abolish the Chilean Senate.

unmaking the government. But one can readily see how more extreme forms can justify much more serious curbs on the legislature.

The second and third justifications lead to a reduction in the powers of the legislature on oligarchical or "realistic" grounds. The oligarchical justification leads either to a second chamber (but, as we saw, this is rarely a strong chamber) or to a monarchical executive. The realistic justification stems from the recognition that legislatures have proved inefficient (one remembers for instance the "vices" described by Lowell) and some degree of streamlining must be introduced. Thus, somewhat paradoxically, all three types of justifications for curbs on the legislature lead to a reduction of the powers of the legislature in favor of the executive. Even where the popular will remains the basis for constitutional arrangements, various constitutional twists lead to various encroachments.

Let us consider how constitutions reduce in practice the powers of the legislature. We have said repeatedly that lawmaking is the means by which legislatures are given a legal say in the decision-making process. At one extreme, therefore, we shall find those countries in which the lawmaking powers are restricted through the use of the referendum, either for ordinary legislation or, if the restriction is weaker, on constitutional matters only (democratic justification). At the other extreme, one will find those countries in which the lawmaking powers of the legislature are restricted by powers given directly to the executive. These latter powers vary and may cover different situations. It may be that, in an emergency, the executive can pass laws without having to refer to the legislature; it may be that the field of legislation is defined restrictively and that the executive can decide alone on other matters at any time; it may be that the executive has some negative powers over legislation, ranging from a right to ask for a second consideration of bills to a complete veto. And in some further cases, as in the United Kingdom, some of the executive powers have been abolished by disuse.

It is not easy to rank these various executive rights "perfectly," but some groupings do emerge. First, at the more "democratic" end, we find 29 countries (a quarter of the universe) where referendums are given some scope for bills, while a further 19 allow referendums for constitutional matters, though in some cases it is possible, if the majority is large enough in the chamber, to avoid the referendum. At the other end, the situation is more confused as one must distinguish between "emergency powers" and powers given for normal times. Emergency powers are commonly allowed; in 58 countries the executive can invoke these powers alone, though some subsequent ratification has to take place in all but eight countries. Under emergency powers, the constitution often gives wide and ill-defined powers to the executive (the best known case being probably that of the Article 16 of the French constitution). Many countries allow "provisional" statutes to be promulgated by this procedure and in 14 countries it is specifically stated that the executive has total freedom. In normal situations the executive often has large powers also. In almost two-thirds of the countries (66) it can send a bill to be reread by the assembly, and in roughly the same number (63) a veto can be exercised, though only in a small minority (10 countries) is this veto final. Various restrictions over fields of activity exist in over half the constitutions (56), covering foreign and even home affairs in 36 of these.

If we exclude independent executive action in the field of foreign affairs (which can be deemed as consistent with the classical theory of legislatures), one can identify four groups of countries. In one group there is no restriction and the legislature is sovereign; in the other three, restrictions stem from popular involvement, executive powers, or both. These restrictions are so widespread that, as Table 4-3 shows, only in about one-third of the countries is the legislature constitutionally supreme in lawmaking, while the situation is obscure in a further 10 to 15 cases. These restrictions exist irrespective of the emergency powers which, as we have seen, are to be found in many countries and irrespective of the veto powers of the executive. Only 17 of the 39 countries which give full lawmaking powers to legislatures do not grant the executive the right to veto bills, and only a dozen do not grant either veto powers or the right to demand second readings.

The general distribution of the decision-making powers of legislatures in the contemporary world is as follows. In a very small minority of cases scattered across the world and including some Communist, Atlantic, and Commonwealth countries, the legislative is supreme. Even in these cases referendums may be allowed in constitutional matters and executives may intervene in emergencies, as in India. In a further 20 to 50 countries the executive has some powers of intervention, but these are mainly negative; it can veto legislation, generally with limitations that stipulate that the legislature has the right to pass its original text at a second deliberation if the majority is large enough. In about 15 to 20 countries there are even greater

Table 4-3.   Restrictions on the Lawmaking Powers of Legislatures

Legislative Referendums	Powers of Executive on Internal Legislation (exclusive of veto)			
	None	*Some*	*Not known*	*Total*
None	39	12	3	54
Allowed for	12	16	1	29
Not known	10	8	7	25
Total	61	36	11	108

executive powers in that the executive can legislate, positively or negatively, on internal matters in fields described in the constitution. At the other extreme, in a further 15 to 20 countries the legislature is restricted because the people have the right to intervene in legislation, as is the case in Switzerland and, in theory at least, in several other countries ranging from Italy to East Germany. Finally, for about 15 countries the powers of the executive are combined with powers given to the people, as has been the case in France since 1958 and, on the basis of the French model, in a number of French-speaking African states.[5] (See Figure 4–1.)

Overall, legislatures of the contemporary world are restricted in their lawmaking role. To argue that legislatures are "all-powerful" and supreme in legislation is simply not true even from a constitutional standpoint. It is therefore not surprising that it should not be true in reality, as we have argued is likely to be the case. Although the strength of legislatures need to be examined in practice, a cross-national study of constitutions is more revealing than is often suggested.

THE CURBS ON THE POWERS OF THE LEGISLATURE OVER THE LIFE OF THE EXECUTIVE

The models of executive-legislative relationships have been repeatedly discussed and referred to since Locke and Montesquieu as the "parliamentary" system and the "presidential" system. Parliamentary systems are said to foster a balanced relationship between executive and legislature: while the legislature can choose the executive, the power of dissolution granted to the executive leaves the ultimate decision in the hands of the people. In the separation of powers or presidential system, on the other hand, the break between executive and legislature is complete and neither proceeds from nor can dismiss the other.

This traditional way of distinguishing between the two systems is more theoretical than real, for the right of dissolution did not exist even in some of the best known "parliamentary" systems. In particular, it was always noted that France did not have a full right of dissolution—but it was generally argued that this was one of the reasons why the French system did not operate "properly." It is also known that a presidential or separation-of-powers system such as that of the United States does not produce full and complete separation, first because of the veto, and second because of the role of the Senate with respect to many presidential appointments. It therefore becomes interesting to examine to what extent the two models are in fact followed in the constitutions of the contemporary world. Indeed, it often has been pointed out that many recent constitutions, and the 1958

[5] The same could be said to be true of the late 1960s in the Central African Republic.

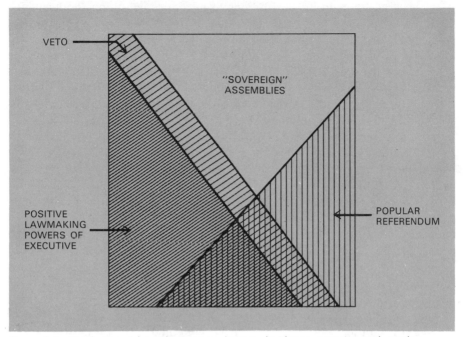

Figure 4–1   Distribution of lawmaking powers between legislature, executive, and people.

French constitution in particular, are "hybrid" in that they organize arrangements which do not properly fit into either of the models.

In order to examine the problem, we need to go somewhat beyond the dichotomy and devise a ranking which would embrace not only the models which create an "equilibrium" between the powers—that is, the presidential and parliamentary models—but also the "unbalanced" models which at both extremes either maintain the supremacy of the executive or give the legislature overriding powers by making the executive dependent on the legislature without weapons of counterattack. The former was known, early in the nineteenth century, as the "constitutional" model and the latter is sometimes described as the "convention" model and is said to exist when the executive is a mere servant of the legislature.

In order to discover, in the reality of constitutions, how the various arrangements are distributed, indicators of executive-legislative strength have to be chosen. The two which are most relevant to these points are the right of censure and the right of dissolution. In the two "equilibrium" models, either both exist at the same time or neither does. In nonequilibrium models the constitution gives the legislature considerable strength if there is a censure but no dissolution; in the converse position, the executive is constitutionally strong. But we can further refine this distinction, because it has become common in constitutions to introduce conditions under which censure or dissolution can occur. The case of the West German constitution, with the "constructive motion of confidence" is very well known indeed; allegedly in order to avoid the difficulties in which the Weimar Republic often found itself as a result of the parties at both extremes combining to overthrow governments, a system was devised making the right of censure difficult to exercise, and at the same time, as is less well known, the dissolution rights were very closely restricted.[6] We therefore can consider not only those cases where dissolution or censure exist or do not exist, but also those intermediate cases where both or either exist in part. From this we can deduce five positions on a continuum of legislative-executive relations, as shown in Table 4–4.

It is noticeable that all the cells are in fact filled, even though some do not include many observations (perhaps in part because a further 16 countries had to be excluded in view of obscurities). Only about half the countries (48) correspond to either "equilibrium" model: this number would be further reduced if we took into account not merely powers to dismiss the executive or the chamber but also powers over legislation, in that—as has always been noted for the United States, for example, the veto cannot be said to follow logically from a strict interpretation of the separation of powers. In another seven countries (West Germany is one of them), the system is also in equilibrium as censure and dissolution are both restricted and thus balance each other. At both extremes, the constitutions of the world organize a number of systems (12 and 11) where one of the "powers" is much superior to the other (with Communist countries typically granting supremacy to the legislature) while, in a number of intermediate cases, either the powers of the executive are not markedly restricted (France is one of them) or the powers of the legislature are fairly large. Thus the theory devised by Locke and Montesquieu has some significant impact, in that it applies to half the countries. On the other hand, it is important to note that it applies to only half of them.

One needs to go further, however, and consider more closely the role of the legislature in these various constitutional models if one is to understand both the reasons for and the characteristics of the spread of the countries along the continuum. For a country to be at the extreme pro-executive end of the continuum, some authority must be vested in the executive, and in particular its head, in order to justify and ultimately maintain this overwhelming executive strength. In relation to second chambers, we noted that the "democratic principle" tended normally to prevail in con-

---

[6] The Bundestag can censure only the Chancellor if it elects a new Chancellor in his place (constructive motion of confidence); the German President can dissolve the Bundestag only in certain circumstances arising from a Cabinet fall.

Table 4–4. Distribution of Countries of the Contemporary World in Relation to Censure and Dissolution Powers

Strong Executive Powers		(3) Both full dissolution and full censure (parliamentary)	(4)	(5) Strong Assembly Powers
← (1) No censure full dissolution	(2) Restrictions on censure full dissolution	27	Restrictions on dissolution full censure	No dissolution full censure →
12	4	Restrictions on dissolution and on censure	2	11
	Restrictions on dissolution no censure	7	Restrictions on censure no dissolution	
	1	Neither dissolution nor censure (presidential)	7	
		21		

(unknown 16)

stitutions, though it could be somewhat thwarted in detail or through the operation of some other principle, such as the equality of representation of the various regions. Similarly, we should expect that the executive will be truly strong only if—and we shall come back to this point in the next chapter —some independent authority is vested in him. This can arise, constitu- tionally at least, either on the basis of heredity and loyalty to a monarch or because a democratic election gives the head of the executive equal status to that of the legislature. Thus in the contemporary world, when a legisla- ture exists, the authority of the head of state arises from three possible sources: the monarchical principle, universal suffrage (or a modified form of universal suffrage such as the election by a fairly large electoral college), and election by the legislature. Constitutions divide fairly evenly between these three models, with universal suffrage being somewhat more common than either of the other two (41 cases versus 32 cases of election by the legislature and 29 monarchies). Thus only a third to a quarter of the legislatures elect the head of state and can therefore be said to be wholly in control of the authority of government.

A number of characteristics are linked to this threefold distinction. Firstly, full rights of dissolution tend to occur primarily in monarchies (this is why it is interesting to examine monarchies even when, as in the United Kingdom, the monarch is merely a symbol), even though in a substantial number of cases (e.g., France), a head of state elected by universal suffrage can also dissolve the legislature and has full powers to do so. As a result, monarchical regimes tend to maintain executive strength more than republican regimes. On the other hand, republics in which the head of state is elected by the chamber are those in which the legislature most commonly has powers over the executive. Secondly, it follows from this division that the parliamentary system, with its "balanced" system of censure and dissolution, exists primarily in monarchies. Thus, had not so many monarchies been maintained, (even if only with a symbolic monarch) we would be confronted, outside presidential systems, with no prevailing model of executive-legislature relationship in the contemporary world, but rather with a number of disjointed and hybrid systems. Curbs on the powers of the legislature over the appointment of the executive would be distributed at random. Locke and Montesquieu prevailed, as shown in Table 4–5, because kings remained in office, but not in power, and became compatible with modern democracies.

The foregoing analysis of constitutions suggests a variety of patterns and indicates that the array is much broader than might have been expected. The models of lawmaking supremacy and the presidential, parliamentary (and possibly convention) models of government are far from being the only constitutional arrangements which exist. Of course, we need to go be-

Table 4–5.   Distribution of "Monarchical," "Universal Suffrage," and Legislature-based Heads of State in the Contemporary World

	Strong Executive (1 & 2)	Equilibrium (3)			Strong Legislature (4 & 5)
		"Parliamentary"	Other	"Presidential"	
Monarchies	6	18	0	1	1
Universal suffrage presidents	7	4	3	17	6
Legislature-based heads of states	4	5	4	3	13
All	17	27	7	21	20

yond these institutional powers and see how far the legislature is able to restrain the executive or how far the executive can, on the contrary, impose its dominance. But the constitutional analysis already paves the way, for we know that there are still many monarchies and that there are many popularly elected presidents. In both cases we can expect some autonomous power and authority for the executive. Moreover, the scatter of systems which give the legislature the right to elect the head of state points to the fact that problems are likely to arise unless some further device (as we know exists in Communist states) reduces markedly the powers of the legislature. Most constitutions organize a democratic base for the assembly; its status is high, but its powers are sometimes trimmed by the constitution itself while the constitution also shows that another authority can limit appreciably the strength of the elected representatives. How far is this strength really reduced and where can assemblies be expected to have saved some of what originally was thought to be their supremacy?

THE CONSTRAINTS ON LEGISLATURES

5

Beyond constitutional variations in powers, limitations on the influence of legislatures depend on the extent to which a variety of constraints operate. These fall naturally into two types. Some, which can be labeled *internal,* stem from the structure of the body itself, or from the characteristics of members; others, which can be labeled *external,* stem primarily from the extent of influence or even coercion which outside elements—mainly the executive—can exercise on the legislature. Constitutional limitations are, in a sense, part of these external constraints: although their complexity suggests that they must be examined separately, their effectiveness depends on the strength of the executive and on its ability to rely on influence and authority.

Executives will not be able to curb the powers of the legislature unless they have enough *authority* to impose these curbs on legislators and on the nation as a whole. If they do not have this authority, demands for increased constitutional strength will arise and might prove to be irresistible. Hence a paradox: those executives which most need to limit the powers of the legislature through constitutional means because they are weakest are in fact precisely the executives which cannot do so because they lack the authority to impose the constitutional curbs. Conversely, those executives which have a very strong authority over the nation and the legislature can afford to appear to give the legislature constitutional powers, because these will not in practice be used. Communist executives do not need to restrict markedly the legal powers of their legislatures. Very strong executives are therefore likely to be found at both ends of the continuum of constitutional powers. (See Figure 5-1.)

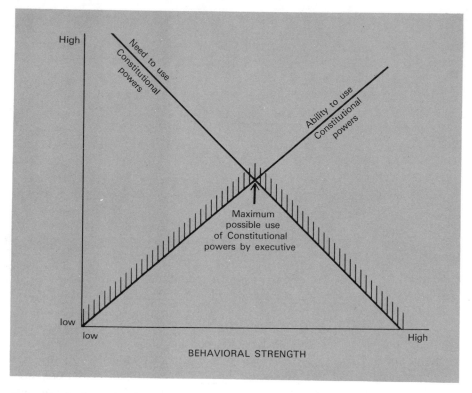

Figure 5-1   Behavioral and constitutional strength of the executive.

INTERNAL CONSTRAINTS ON LEGISLATURES

We saw in Chapter 2 that legislators can be involved in matters ranging from particular to general. Even if no external constraints were exercised on a legislature, its ability to handle problems would depend on its internal organization. If we further assume that the technical complexity of problems increases more than proportionately as the polity becomes more advanced socio-economically, we might even expect the effectiveness of legislatures to decrease as we move from underdevloped to developed polities.

Three types of internal constraints are unavoidably at play. First, legislatures need time to examine problems. Time should be considered not merely in absolute terms, but relative to the population which the legislature serves. The more legislators for a given number of electors, the more time each legislator has to handle constituents' problems. On this score, large countries are at a disadvantage, in part because of an obvious reluctance to let legislatures grow beyond about six hundred to seven hundred members, and this rule has a particularly strong effect on the legislatures of the largest countries. The legislatures of small countries have a much higher ratio of legislators per head of population than the legislatures of large countries.

Geographical variations, as well as what appear to be ideological differences, also must be taken into account here. The ratio of legislators to population is highest in Communist states and lowest in the Third World. Atlantic countries occupy an intermediate position, but, inasmuch as Atlantic countries tend to have two chambers, they score high overall. In the Third World, the ratio is lower in Asia than in Africa and Latin America—particularly in the latter region, if second chambers are included. The higher ratios in the more developed societies thus may help to compensate for the fact that problems are more technically complex and constituent pressures are likely to be more numerous in socioeconomically advanced countries than in other polities.

The time spent by legislators on their job is of course not solely a function of the size of the legislature per head of population. Firstly, legislators may be more or less helped in their task by assistants and secretaries, and they can thus multiply their activities. Given that legislatures do not grow in proportion to population increases, we should expect the number of assistants to go up, even for the same amount of complexity of the socioeconomic system, if legislators of a given country are to continue to cope to the same extent with that country's problems. Secondly, the amount of time which legislators can and do devote to the activities of the legislature varies. They may be full-time or part-time legislators. One would expect members to become increasingly full-time as populations increase, but other factors might act against this trend: not only the pay and conditions of service, but the norms of the political system may tend to reduce the time spent by members on the legislature's business. If it is commonly believed that it is good for legislators to have other activities because this keeps them in touch with the country (as has often been claimed in the United Kingdom, for instance), then the time spent by the legislator on public affairs may remain relatively low.

A second type of internal constraint relates to political and technical competence. Politically, legislators should be alert to problems and willing to act on any question, whether detailed, intermediate, or general. In principle this type of political competence may be acquired during a prior political career, yet the extent to which this prior training takes place varies markedly. Where the sociopolitical system is closed, where ascriptive tendencies prevail, and where it is possible for someone to become a member of the legislature at a very early age merely by having in some figurative manner, "inherited" the post, the political skills of the legislators are likely to be lower, on average, than where the members have had to exercise these skills through a long series of political battles, probably beginning at the local level, prior to joining the legislature. Moreover—and this is the argument commonly made for having part-time legislators—it is essential that the legislator should not be cut off from the rest of the population if he is to exercise his communication function effectively; the development of full-time legislators may lead to a greater divorce between members and constituents and to a reduction in at least this aspect of the legislator's competence.

Legislators also must be technically competent in the various fields of government. Indeed, ideally, they should be competent in all matters of public interest, an impossible goal to achieve and an increasingly unrealistic one as the polity becomes more complex. Yet some degree of technical competence must be obtained, for legislators with low competence are likely to be more ineffective as the complexity of the matters they handle increases. Legislators must be able to understand problems and to understand the way in which these problems lead to given types of outputs from the administrative system. For this they need to be trained, either on the spot or before coming to the house. In principle, therefore, we should expect new members to be rather ineffective unless their prior training has helped. Overall, the question of the types of men, of their views and interests, of their general involvement in the matters of the legislature, as well as the range of interests represented is therefore of some importance in determining the competence of members of an assembly.

 Thirdly, the efficiency of the legislature and of the legislators depends on the extent to which the assembly as a whole provides an infrastructure which helps members and increases their competence. This covers a wide variety of arrangements, procedures, and technical supports. At one extreme, they relate to the techniques of debate and decision making; in particular, if procedures alter very slowly despite changes in functions or changes in the relative importance of each function, the legislature may be very ineffective, and this may in turn have some impact on the morale of legislators and their sense of efficacy. At the other extreme, arrangements relate to the technical supports which are given to legislators. Inasmuch as legislators cannot be universally competent, and inasmuch as their competence is likely to decrease as the size and complexity of the country increases, supports which are given to legislators must become increasingly professional and technical and the general environment provided by the assembly must be such that legislators are quickly socialized and permanently spurred into increasing their competence gearing themselves to the intricacies of the administrative system. This is why committees are of considerable importance to the development of well equipped legislative activities, for they are the main means by which the legislature can help legislators to tackle technical problems and, indeed, to become aware of the nature of these problems. While enabling members to be specialized in a variety of ways, they also provide those who are not competent in a particular field with the knowledge of the points where they can obtain this technical information. Even where committees are not directly influential, they are an important element of the socialization of members in contemporary legislatures.

EXTERNAL CONSTRAINTS: THE STRENGTH OF THE EXECUTIVE For the executive to be able to reduce the influence of the legislature, it must have, as was said in the introduction to this chapter, some independent authority, whatever constitutional curbs are at its disposal. This independent strength can come broadly from two sources, which can be labeled "legitimacy" or "authority," on the one hand, and "dominance" or coercion on the other. No regime and no executive is entirely legitimate in the sense that it can dispense wholly with coercion, but no regime can maintain itself for any length of time without some element of legitimacy. We can distinguish these two poles in the form of a contrast between "imposed" and "natural" systems, with real-world polities lying between these two extremes and, indeed, occupying different positions at different moments in time.

External constraints exercised on legislatures by executives depend on a complex combination of these two factors. First, the more the regime is imposed, the more the legislature is likely to be subservient to the executive, as the executive is not likely to tolerate manifestations of independence on the part of the legislature any more than on the part of any other body. Where the regime is markedly imposed, the legislature's scope for action is therefore likely to be markedly restricted, both in terms of the range of its activities and in terms of the extent to which it will be able to discuss each problem. If the legislature goes beyond the acceptable bounds, legislators will be coerced (for instance through trials and imprisonment), but of course the threat of coercion often will be sufficient to keep them within bounds.

This type of dominance is rarely used in this naked fashion. Influence through various forms of "authority" is more common and is likely to be as effective in the long run. For such an influence to exist, the executive must have a legitimacy of its own. Inasmuch as the legislature represents the population, the executive's legitimacy can emerge either because of a bond of allegiance other than popular representation or because popular representation is divided between the executive and the legislature.

One can distinguish four different types of situations in which the executive is in a position to limit markedly the role of the legislature. The first corresponds to the traditional or semi-traditional regime, where a monarch has the loyalty of large segments of the population. In this case the conflict which is likely to arise between executive and legislature corresponds to the opposition between traditional and modern elements in the polity at large. This type of conflict occurred very often in nineteenth-century Europe.

In a second type of case, a leader may have a personal appeal such that the population is prepared to follow him and indeed that the rest of the political elite (including the legislature) effectively depends on the leader for its political survival. A common example is that of the new country where a charismatic leader succeeds in bringing about independence and thereby acquires a considerable following. In such a case, conflicts between legislature and executive will be limited and the legislature's subservience may be as marked as where there is coercion. To the extent that this is so, actual coercion will not be needed, although in practice a mixture of coercion and personal allegiance to the leader is likely to be found. If there is conflict, the legislature may tend to represent traditional or sectional interests (for instance, the chiefs in a developing country), and in this case the opposition between executive and legislature is not likely to be, as in the previous case, an opposition in which the executive represents tradition, but the reverse.

Thirdly, the strength of the executive may come from the existence of national political structures with which the population identifies. The main structure of this type is, of course, the political party. If the population identifies with one or more political parties, the leader or leaders of these parties will have indirect authority derived from the party and thus will be in a position to exercise influence over the legislators. Indeed, the members of the legislature are likely to owe their election to party selection. To the extent that this is the case, the executive can "control" them, usually without having to go to the extreme of threats of expulsion or actual expulsion.

Parties are not the only type of national structure from which the authority of the executive can proceed. Various types of groups—e.g., religious groups, the bureaucracy, and the army—can form the nuclei or bases of an executive. But parties are the only institutions which consciously and commonly constitute a channel of communication between people and executive. The other structures are more likely to bypass the people altogether, although parties, too, may have little contact with the population. To the extent that parties or other structures have a following independent from the legislature, they can transmit to the executive an authority which is also independent from the legislature.

Fourthly, the executive may be at least equal, if not superior, to the legislature if the legislature cannot control the existence of the executive, as when the constitution specifies that the executive is directly elected by the people. Constitutional arrangements which provide for a popularly elected president thus also provide for at least some authority for the executive, as was suggested in the previous chapter. The legislature may be relatively stronger than in the other three situations just analyzed, but the example of the United States shows that the presidential system, by itself, can provide the executive with a not inconsiderable amount of influence.

FORMS OF EXECUTIVE INFLUENCE AND THE STRENGTH OF LEGISLATURES

Let us examine somewhat more closely the effect on the role of the legislature of the variables introduced in the preceding section. Clearly, the legislature will be strongest in a legitimate political system which is neither presidential nor monarchical, has weak party structures, and has a low level of personalization of the leadership.

1. In a strongly traditional system, where the authority of the monarch is considerable, the legislature will be either weak or in conflict with the executive. If the monarch has retained the allegiance of most of the population, the legislature will be weak—indeed, there may not even be a legislature. As support for representative government increases, the legislature might become stronger, but conflicts also will become more frequent, so that the monarch may be tempted to exercise coercion to maintain his supremacy. Thus legislatures of traditional systems range from weak to very weak and are subjected to manipulation by the executive.

2. Legislatures are also weak in regimes based on the strong personal appeal of a leader. This is the situation which prevails in many developing countries. In these cases there may or may not also be a party system; if there is one it typically will be a single party. Indeed a hereditary monarch also may have some personal appeal, as was the case in Cambodia under Sihanouk as well as in Iran and even Morocco. The stronger the personal appeal of the leader, the weaker the legislature. But personal appeal is, by its very nature, subject to rapid fluctuations over time (more so, for instance, than hereditary allegiance). As a result, the strength of the legislature varies appreciably in these systems.

3. Military regimes are likely to coincide with very weak legislatures. Indeed, as the military does not typically provide a link between the people and the executive independently from the legislature and is thus unable to exert pressure from the inside, coercion is likely to be high and the legislature is often dispensed with. Military regimes constitute the large majority of the nonmonarchical cases where there is no legislature. However, the military regimes are not always "pure": there may be a dose of "monarchical" legitimacy, as in Thailand, and in these cases the legitimacy of the system may be greater and the legislature may be maintained. Moreover, because of their very inability to influence the population directly, military rulers progressively "civilianize" their regimes by creating a party, unless they consider themselves as merely transitional and hand over power fairly

quickly to civilian leaders, as in Ghana in the late 1960s. The civilianization process leads normally to the creation both of a party and of constitutional institutions—in particular a legislature—although there may be a deliberate lag to ensure that the party will have a firm base and will play a leading part in the elections. (Egypt followed this path in the early 1960s and Indonesia and Zaïre appeared to be engaged in a similar process in the 1970s.) Finally, special circumstances may allow for the maintenance of the legislature if the justification for the military regime can be found on other grounds, such as civil war or guerilla warfare (as in Cambodia). Pure military regimes are not well equipped to cope directly with a legislature, the distaste which military rulers tend to have for assemblies being precisely evidence for this inability to manipulate the institution from the inside.

(4.) Perhaps the most interesting and varied situation is that where constraints on the legislature stem from the party system. Because party systems differ widely and are often in a state of flux, the role of the legislature also can differ widely. The party system can combine with either a highly imposed system or a legitimate regime, the party being the main instrument of imposition in the first case and the means by which the various sections, groups, and ideologies, express themselves in the second. Where the system is imposed through the party, the main channel of communication also will tend to be the party and the activities of the legislature will be confined mainly to "symbolic" and "educative" functions, as tends to be the case in Communist systems. As imposition decreases, the real influence of the legislature will increase, as can be seen in some of the Eastern European Communist states, in particular Yugoslavia. Thus, where party imposition is strongest, the legislature can be even weaker than in monarchical systems or in regimes with a high personalization of the leadership.

The legislature is stronger in legitimate systems based on a party system, but even here variations occur. The strength of the executive depends essentially, as we saw, on the extent to which the party constitutes a direct link between executive and people, even though constitutional limitations on the legislature may add to this executive strength. If the development of the polity is natural and if the bases of support are popular rather than monarchical, the configuration of the party system will depend on the group structures in the polity. We cannot, for instance, posit that the party system will be *national* rather than sectional; nor can we know *a priori* how many large to medium sized parties will characterize the polity —that is, whether the system will or will not be highly *fractionalized*. Yet these two factors—national versus sectional parties, and a simple versus a fractionalized party system—have an impact on the strength of the legislature. The more nationalized and the less fractionalized the parties are, the more the executive is likely to be strong. If the parties are truly national (as in the United Kingdom, for example), members of the legislature will be selected by the party and the party leadership and combinations between legislators are unlikely to occur. In these cases, discipline will be strong. If there is one dominant party or a majority party, as in the United Kingdom or Sweden, combinations between parties will be rare or impossible. The strength of the leadership of such a dominant party will be large and the executive will not depend much on the legislature for its maintenance in power and for its action, even if the system is "liberal" and the party system "natural."

If, on the contrary, the nationalization of the parties is not as marked or if the fractionalization of the parties is greater, the strength of the legislature will increase. Whatever the degree of fractionalization, a decrease in the nationalization of the party system will lead to a decrease in the strength of the executive, as can be seen in the United States. Fractionalization begins to have an impact on the strength of the executive beyond the point where there is no majority party, and this impact increases with the number of significant parties, particularly when none of them is appreciably larger than the others (as can be seen in Belgium, the Netherlands, or pre-1958 France). However nationalized the party system may be, a highly fractionalized party system (one in which the legislature is composed of a number of parties of about the same size) will lead to the legislature's being relatively influential.

The type of party system to be found in a polity therefore has a considerable effect on the influence of the legislature. Where the system is imposed, legislatures will range from very weak to weak; they will be weakest if there is large imposition provided by a party and somewhat less weak where personal leadership combines with party influence. Where the system has developed naturally, the legislature is likely to be weak if the nationalization of the parties is high and the degree of fractionalization low; if the converse occurs, the legislature is likely to be strong, although this may lead to considerable instability through lack of leadership, so that the regime as a whole may not be in a position to survive. Where the parties are less nationalized, even if fractionalization is low, the assembly will be fairly strong; indeed, the effect is probably smoother and more continuous than that of fractionalization, because the latter does not affect party discipline while the former does. Thus, if fractionalization increases while nationalization remains constant and high, the executive may remain strong, at least until the party system is so fractionalized that combinations of majorities become numerous and interchangeable.

Internal limitations, the existence of a separate source of authority, and, in some cases, constitutional curbs all lead to the reduction of the legislature's direct and positive role in many of the nation's affairs. In large numbers of countries, this makes it possible for legislatures to be so weak that they have little influence; indeed, at the limit, the legislature may be banned. But we know that the theoretical rights of legislatures in fact go much beyond what the legislatures actually could have achieved, and the proof is that where legislatures truly predominate, where party constraints did not sufficiently exist, where the logic of internal limitations did not lead legislators to agree to the executive's upper hand, the period of rule by the assembly has tended to be short. The executive's upper hand is thus not, by itself, detrimental to the healthy development of assembly influence; it is inevitable and indeed quite positive. What is needed is to see how far, within this context, legislatures remain active, to what extent they achieve changes in the polity by influencing leaders. We need to examine activities as well as influence, not hold as axiomatic that assemblies are reduced to very little role, but seeing whether and how across the world they vary in the scope of this role and how far it is possible to distinguish between those assemblies which clearly do not achieve much and those which do seem to make a mark on the life of the polity.

THE GENERAL PATTERN OF ACTIVITIES OF LEGISLATURES

6

The constraints under which legislatures operate are naturally reflected in the extent of their activities. To be sure, activity is not coextensive with influence. But activities constitute an indicator of influence, for it is unlikely that an assembly will be very active if the executive is adamant to reduce its strength, nor will it remain inactive if it is fairly independent.

Although the measurement of activity poses less difficulties than the measurement of influence, the information which is readily available remains very scanty on both scores. There is no full-scale survey of even the most elementary type of activity—namely, the number of days of sittings of the world's legislatures. For the purpose of this analysis, inferences will be drawn from about thirty countries (nearly a third of the countries with legislatures) for which some literature exists or for which debates were accessible. These countries are scattered across the world, from the Atlantic area to Asia and Africa and from Eastern Communist states to Latin America. Generalizations are therefore possible for many of the activities and they constitute at least a preliminary guide to the patterns of behavior of the world's legislatures.[1]

The activities surveyed constitute, nonetheless, only a limited segment of assembly activities. They concern mainly activities on the floor of the house, with only partial investigations into committee work. But by considering the extent to which legislatures meet, by examining how they distribute their work, by seeing whether committees are well developed, and by attempting to assess whether debates are sullen or lively, we begin to catch the flavor and content of the work and thus prepare the ground for a better understanding of their overall role.

[1] The list and characteristic activities of these countries is given in Appendix II.

THE YEARLY PATTERN OF LEGISLATIVE SESSIONS

As we said earlier, there is no general survey of even the pattern of sittings of legislatures. We know about extreme cases. The Supreme Soviet of the Soviet Union meets a few days every year, while the British House of Commons sits for five days a week for about thirty weeks and the United States Congress for about the same number of days. Less is known about other countries. But from the survey of the countries mentioned earlier, the United Kingdom and the Soviet Union do indeed seem to be extreme or very near extreme cases, East Germany being seemingly at the very end of the queue with a total of three meetings for the whole of the year 1970, appreciably less than, for instance, Poland and Hungary. No legislature seems to have met during more days than the United States Congress or the British and Candian Houses, and the British House of Commons met for more hours than any other legislature by a very large margin. The other legislatures are spread fairly evenly along the range of both hours and days of sittings. The daily sitting tends to grow longer as the number of daily sittings increases, though some countries are appreciably lower than the regression line—Senegal, Venezula, and the United States in particular. (See Figure 6–1.)

A relationship apparently exists between "liberal-democracy" and the number of days and hours of sittings. East Germany (but not Yugoslavia) is at one extreme and Atlantic countries are at the other, though the latter are scattered over a wide range. One-party systems (Tunisia, Senegal, but not Kenya) and systems where one party is very dominant (Singapore, Madagascar) tend in general to score fairly low on this quantitative measure, whereas systems with more than one party of a balanced two-party or multi-dominant kind (India, Latin American countries) tend to score high or relatively high.

Two further factors have to be taken into account, however. The first concerns the spread of the sittings throughout the year. Clearly, at both extremes, the matter is of little import or goes without saying: the 160 sittings of the British Parliament will necessarily be spread fairly evenly throughout the year; and if the three meetings of the East German Popular Chamber are spread or concentrated, the matter is probably of little significance. But chambers which meet between forty and eighty times a year have two different patterns. One is the French pattern, which also characterizes Latin America, in which the chamber meets for extended periods, even if this means not sitting for more than a few days in a given week or even month. The French chamber meets for six months during the year, although it only meets for about sixty to seventy sittings, or an average of ten days per month (indeed, often much less, as the autumn budgetary session is much more crowded than the other). Venezuela is an extreme case

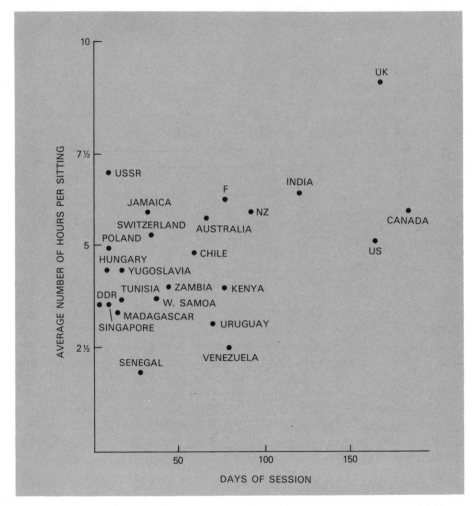

Figure 6–1   Average deviation of sittings in some of the world's legislatures.

in its low average length of daily sittings, which are often of about one hour only. At the other extreme, the Swiss chamber meets for three concentrated periods of about two weeks each, during which the chamber meets almost every day, and for long sittings during these days. Many Commonwealth countries follow the same pattern; in Kenya, for instance, the chamber did not meet between early November and the end of May; in Zambia, after April 1969, it met only for a few days in July and a few days at the end of September.

The existence of these two models suggests a difference in the type (and possibly extent) of control which can be exercised by the chamber on the government. If months pass without the chamber's meeting, even though in theory the chamber may well be "recalled," the practice is that the government is not in fact supervised in its daily activities. The legislature is probably deemed to be, and in fact essentially concentrates on being, a "lawmaking" agency, whether or not it follows closely the lead of the government. Where, as in Latin America, the chamber tends more to be in continuous or at least regular session, the control of the executive is likely to be closer.

The second point relates to the extent to which the average member is in a position to participate in the debates of the chamber. We noted earlier that, in terms of overall meeting time, Latin American countries scored higher than African countries. However, the situation becomes appreciably altered if the amount of time per member is calculated. On this basis, the countries analyzed in the survey vary markedly. (See Table 6–1.) At the bottom, East Germany and the Soviet Union give a tiny amount of time to each of their members (one or two minutes). At the top, two countries, New Zealand and Jamaica, give over four hours. In between, the bulk of the countries give between half an hour and 140 minutes, with the countries in the highest group all belonging to the Commonwealth; indeed, no country of the Commonwealth, except Singapore, gives less than an hour and a half on average to each of its members.

Table 6-1. Time per Member in Contemporary Legislatures (in minutes)

Atlantic	Commonwealth	Latin American	French-Speaking	Communist
	New Zealand 415 Jamaica 245 Australia 190 W. Samoa 155 Canada 150 UK 140			
		Uruguay 120		
US 110	Zambia 105 Kenya 100 India 90	Chile 105		
		Venezuela 65		
France 60 Switzerland 50				Yugoslavia 50
			Tunisia 40 Senegal 40 Madagascar 35	
	Singapore 35			
				USSR 7 Hungary 7 Poland 5 DDR 1

Three conclusions follow. The first is that Communist countries (except Yugoslavia) divide very sharply from the rest of the world; the meetings of these assemblies clearly do not allow for any form of debate for the average member; he is there to listen, but not to talk. This does not happen to anywhere near the same extent in the other one-party States. Secondly, Commonwealth countries give appreciably more opportunities to their members than other countries, whether or not these countries belong to the "developed" world and indeed even regardless of whether these countries are one-party systems or near one-party systems. Th single exception here is Singapore. Latin American countries do not score as high on this index as Commonwealth countries, and even Chile has a lower score. Thirdly, it becomes interesting to examine whether the nature of the debate and the type of participation differs in countries with low or average scores from what it is in countries which score fairly high. It seems plausible to assume that the extent of disagreements will be in Madagascar or Singapore, or that only a small proportion of the members have an opportunity to participate in the legislature. It becomes important, therefore, to turn to the activities of the legislatures and to the nature of individual participation.

THE DISTRIBUTION OF FLOOR ACTIVITIES

We noted in Chapter 2 that legislatures could be involved in a whole variety of activities, detailed and general, though lawmaking was likely in fact to play a very large part because of the theory of the legislature's role. But the British House of Commons does spend the first hour of every day on question time and engages in a variety of other debates which are not concerned with legislation. Do similar activities take place in other legislatures, and do those assemblies which meet much less frequently than the United Kingdom Parliament divide their work proportionately in the same fashion?

THE OVERALL DISTRIBUTION OF TIME

Table 6–2 gives an impression of the overall distribution of time among the countries which were studied on the basis of a division between legislation, debates of a general character, financial matters, and question time. For a few countries, in particular Latin American countries, the financial session could not be studied and the picture is therefore somewhat distorted. Moreover, in Yugoslavia much of the discussion attributed to debates relates in fact to the economic plan, which can be construed to relate either to the budget or to legislation. Generally, the figures should not be taken to be more than a rough indication, given that only one year was studied for most of the countries.

Table 6-2. Distribution of Floor Activities (in percentage)

	Lawmaking	Finance	Debates (general)	Questions
UK	40	20	32	8
Australia	30	25	35	10
India	23	25	28	15
France	43	35	8	4
Singapore	72	3	22	3
Yugoslavia	20	17	60	3
Chile (excluding budget session)	63	?	20	17
Switzerland	71	18	5	0
Uruguay (excluding budget session)	40	?	40	5
Madagascar	70	25	3	2
Senegal	66	13	18	3
East Germany	67	33	0	0

Nevertheless, some conclusions emerge fairly clearly. First, question time plays a large part in Commonwealth countries but not only in these countries. Interestingly, even the Singapore legislature, which met only nine times throughout the year, devoted a substantial proportion of its time to questions (in fact more than any other country in percentage). Latin American countries, particularly Chile, also use the question period to a fairly large extent; the procedure exists also in Uruguay but is less regularly practiced. Secondly, considerable variations exist in the amount of time devoted by the legislatures to general debates. In a number of countries, including Atlantic countries (France and Switzerland), debates play a very small part in the activities of the legislature, both of these chambers spending almost the whole of their time on what might be termed "traditional" matters such as legislation and finance. On the other hand, several Commonwealth countries and Latin American countries are involved in a variety of debates; in Chile debates often take place on the technical question of the decision to allow a minister to go abroad, this being an occasion for a foreign affairs debate or for a debate on social or economic problems.

Thirdly, the less the assembly meets, the more legislation seems to play a part in the activities of the chamber. This is no more than a trend, admittedly, and conclusions are somewhat obscured by the absence of data for financial legislation in Chile and Uruguay. But, among non-Communist countries, those which meet least spend over two-thirds of their time on legislation, whereas, except for Switzerland, none of the countries which meet for longer hours devote as high a percentage of their time to lawmaking. In the Swiss case, legislation proper only takes about 35 to 40 percent of the time of the National Council, but another quarter of the total time is concerned with federal regulations which have also to be approved by the chamber. This procedure reflects the fairly tight control exercised by the Swiss legislature over the Federal Council, and therefore justifies to some extent the use of the phrase "convention government" to characterize the Swiss system, although this does not mean that the initiative lies in fact with the legislature. All other assemblies which meet fairly frequently tend to give a much more modest place to legislation, the percentage being even as low as 23 percent in India and 30 percent in Australia. At the other extreme, East Germany devotes a very high percentage of its time to legislation. The case of Yugoslavia is complex since, as we noted, much of the discussion during the year of analysis was devoted to the five-year plan and could therefore be deemed to correspond either to financial matters or to legislation. In East Germany, however, the discussion on legislation did not take place on details and was therefore not very different from a general debate.

The following pattern therefore emerges. First, the time spent by legislatures in public sittings is so low in some countries that meetings seem mainly to constitute occasions for statements from the executive and for expressions of support by some of the chamber's leaders. Second, for another group of countries in which the total time is short, most of it is devoted to legislation and almost the whole time is devoted to legislation and finance, except for Singapore, in which, as in other Commonwealth countries, a large part of the sittings is reserved for questions. The rest of the countries do not spend more than between 25 and 45 percent of their sittings on lawmaking, but the allocation of the rest of the time varies and they divide into two groups on this matter. Commonwealth countries are the only ones which distribute their activities fairly evenly between general debates and question time, while others—Latin American countries in particular—do not seem to distinguish as sharply between matters of general concern (debates) and more particular matters (questions). Overall, however, matters other than lawmaking play a significant part in legislatures which have a high level of activity.

THE NATURE OF THE LEGISLATIVE DEBATE

The amount of time spent on laws varies considerably both relatively and absolutely. In order to assess whether debates on legislation involve real discussion, we need to consider three further indicators, one of which, the time spent by each legislator on laws, we already encountered, while the other two relate to the number of laws passed by the legislature and the apparent overall importance of these laws.

Given that, on balance, the legislatures which tend to meet rather less are also those in which the percentage of time devoted to laws is the largest,

Table 6-3.   Average Time per Legislator on Debates on Legislation (minutes per year)

Australia ⎫ UK ⎬ Chile ⎭	about 55	India	about 20
		Madagascar	about 15
		Yugoslavia	about 10-15
Uruguay	about 50	East Germany	about 7
Switzerland	about 35		
France ⎫ Senegal ⎬ Singapore ⎭	about 25		

the average amount of time during which each legislator can participate in the debates on the laws which are being discussed does not vary as markedly as the average meeting time per member. If we exclude the countries at both ends (East Germany, New Zealand, and Jamaica) the overall meeting time per member varies from 22 minutes (Madagascar) to 160 minutes (Australia), or roughly 1 to 7; but in terms of time per deputy devoted to legislation, the variations are at most 1 to 4, from 14 minutes in Madagascar to 55 minutes in the United Kingdom. Indeed, Madagascar appears to be unique in being so ungenerous in the time it gives its deputies to debate legislation. All the other countries appear to fall into two groups: those which give about 25 minutes per legislator and those which give about double that amount. France, Senegal, and India fall into the first category while the United Kingdom, Australia, Switzerland (excluding delegated legislation), and the Latin American countries (if one assumes that the budget does not take much of the time of the legislators) fall into the latter. It is therefore wrong to suggest that countries of the Third World give appreciably less time to their legislators to debate laws than do countries of the Atlantic world. Indeed, it is interesting to note that France, as a result of the 1958 constitution, unquestionably has given to its legislators much less time to debate laws than many other Atlantic countries, whereas India, which scores high in terms of the total of time of meetings, scores low in terms of the time during which each member can participate in lawmaking. Although some differences remain in the extent to which individual legislators have opportunities to make their views known on the laws of their country, it is more in the extent to which they can discuss other matters publicly that differences are marked between the various legislatures.

The situation is altered considerably, however, when the number of laws passed by the legislature is taken into consideration. Clearly, there are vast cultural differences in the amount of legislative output: it is normally noted that very few laws are passed in the Communist countries, though there has recently been a tendency toward a slight increase, as in the USSR.

But the difference emerges clearly in the sample of countries examined here, for East Germany and the Soviet Union are at the very bottom; only four laws were passed in East Germany, whereas the United States House of Representatives is at the other extreme, with over three hundred laws passed in 1968. The other countries are fairly evenly scattered. A number of countries (Singapore, Yugoslavia, Kenya, and Switzerland, though delegated legislation perhaps should be added in the Swiss case) passed about fifteen to twenty laws; in another group of countries (United Kingdom, Australia, and India) about fifty to sixty were passed. A further group, which includes France and Uruguay, passed between 120 and 150 bills during one year, while in Sweden, Costa Rica, and the Philippines over two hundred bills were passed.

It follows that the amount of time at the disposal of each member *for each bill* shows much greater variations than the amount of time at the disposal of each member for the whole of the lawmaking process. Kenyan legislators had most time at their disposal. At the other extreme, French and American legislatures gave their members scarcely more than ten to fifteen seconds, and, given the small number of bills which they were involved in, legislators in the East German Popular Chamber found themselves scarcely less well off. Clearly, two general remarks have to be made. First, the crude number of bills passed is not, as such, an index of the activity in which legislators are involved: it is well known, for instance, that United States congressmen are involved in a whole variety of bills of a personal or individual type which have little to do with policy and are perhaps, in many ways, to be assimilated either with questions or with the passage of outputs of a detailed character, a point to which we shall come again in Chapter 8. French legislators are concerned with the passage of a whole variety of bills relating to international agreements; in 1966, about thirty of the bills passed by the French National Assembly related to agreements, often of a minor kind, with a variety of countries. The same pattern can be found in Senegal. Yet, despite these differences, and irrespective of the cultural or institutional constraints which lead to the passage of bills of a peculiar type, the output of laws varies markedly from country to country.

Second, these variations in the time which each member could participate in each bill show, at least negatively, that it is not the case that countries of the Third World give their members fewer opportunities to speak than other countries. Even though many French and United States bills are of limited importance and even though the figure of fifteen seconds per member per bill reflects this limited importance, it is still the case that each member has only limited opportunities to participate even on the more important laws. By contrast, the much smaller Singapore legislature gives its members reasonable opportunities, even though it meets infrequently. We started from the impression that meetings were relatively rare in many countries; we noted that countries where meetings were infrequent tended to place a greater emphasis on legislation; we noted that, as a result, members from these legislatures were at less of a disadvantage than might have been expected. In fact, when we consider each bill which is passed, we have to conclude that many legislatures which meet frequently do not give their members greater opportunities than those which meet infrequently: on those bills which are being discussed by the legislature, these legislatures may give opportunities to participate which are equal to or even greater than the opportunities available in legislatures which meet more frequently but where more legislation is "processed."

The nature and importance of these bills should be examined more closely, however. We noted already that seemingly large variations existed, in that the United States and French legislatures, for example, become involved in matters which might not rank as "bills" in some other countries and which therefore appear to load legislators more than would otherwise be the case. Moreover, although a legislature such as that of Singapore gives reasonable opportunities to members to speak on each bill which is being discussed, it could be that this is because the bills which are discussed cover only a very small part of the area of government. If bills are few, it would seem to follow either that the government decides on many matters on its own or that very little change takes place in the polity. We already encountered this problem in Chapter 3 and we cannot hope, with the limited amount of research which has been undertaken in the determination of indicators of change, to do more than convey a general impression of the large variations which appear to exist from one country to another.

In some polities, laws seem to cover a very limited number of questions. The most extreme case in the countries studied is that of Singapore, where about half the total time devoted to legislation in one year related to one bill, and that bill was concerned with the reform of abortion laws; there was little or no discussion on social or economic problems, for other bills related to criminal procedure, professional engineers, and so forth. In Madagascar or Senegal, much of the legislation related to matters of a private character or to law and order (creation of a national police corps, for instance), although questions of a social or economic kind (for example creation of a corps of technical teachers and of a national fund for social aid) were touched on more than in Singapore. Laws in Latin American and in some Third World Commonwealth countries seem to be somewhat more important, though here, too, many were relatively trivial. A close study of the legislation passed in five countries during a session suggested that the average importance of bills varied appreciably; given that the number of bills passed also varied markedly, the total weight of legislation, as measured by its importance, seemed to show considerable differences, as shown in Table 6–4.

Table 6-4.   Importance of Legislation in Five Countries*

	Average Importance of Bills (five-point scale 1-5)	Total Weight of Bills (average importance × no. of bills)
UK (1966-67)	3.2	313.6
Ireland (1965)	3.1	105.4
Sweden (1966)	2.1	598.5
France (1966)	1.3	191.1
India (1966	3.1	158.1

Adapted from J. Blondel et al., "Legislative Behavior: Some Steps towards a Cross-National Measurement," Government and Opposition (Winter 1969-70), pp. 75 and 76.

It seems that legislation tends to become more trivial, or is more concentrated on a limited number of fields of government, as one moves toward legislatures which meet infrequently. The conclusions are therefore twofold: on the one hand, legislators in countries of the Third World have opportunities to participate in lawmaking on a scale which is not markedly different from and can even be better than that of legislators in the Atlantic area, even where there is a single-party system or a near single-party system; on the other hand, this legislation tends to cover a limited number of fields and is generally less important than in countries where the total amount of time devoted to lawmaking is larger and where each member has limited opportunities to debate on these important bills. Depending on how we look at the matter, we can say either that legislators in many Third World countries can participate more carefully in legislation or that these legislatures are more concerned with trivia, even though the more important matters which are discussed elsewhere are likely to be pushed through the legislature.

THE CHARACTER AND EXTENT OF THE COMMITTEE SYSTEM

Committees seem so natural to the existence and working of many legislatures—in particular the United States Congress—that it is difficult to believe that assemblies could have worked for a long time without organized committees, and indeed that the whole idea of a committee system developed piecemeal and without a clearcut determination of the functions of these bodies. In the United States, the committee system started mainly to expedite bills, because it seemed impossible to do the work in the whole chamber.[2] In European countries, the development of committees in the

[2] Lord Bryce, *The American Commonwealth* (London: Macmillan & Co., Ltd., 1888), I, 205. There were five committees in the House of Representatives in 1802 and fifty-four in 1888.

nineteenth century was largely ad hoc: it seemed natural to distribute bills to sections of the assembly, but it did not appear necessary to organize these sections on the basis of any party principle or on the basis of any subject. This is why the House of Commons in Britain still reflects in some ways the characteristics of an assembly of the late nineteenth century, for it has kept, and with few modifications, arrangements about the distribution of work to committees which were characteristic of most countries at that time. It is followed in this by some Commonwealth countries.

By a process of gradual development and imitation, however, most of the legislatures of the world have tended to move toward a pattern of "hard-core" of specialized committees which correspond to the major departments of the government. Having started in Western Europe and North America in the nineteenth century, the process extended gradually to new countries after World War II. Latin American countries and French-speaking African countries, for instance, tend to have a dozen or so committees which cover each of the main sectors of public activity; Communist countries have moved in the same direction as a result of a considerable increase in the number of committees in the 1960s.[3] The main exception to this pattern is provided by the United Kingdom and a number of Commonwealth countries. (Canada, however, follows fairly closely the American model.) In the United Kingdom, for instance, bills are sent, in principle at least, to the first available body among the six legislative committees which exist. In practice, however, the membership of these committees has come to be increasingly specialized and members tend to move from one committee to another on the basis of the type of field covered by each bill. The specialization of the men is thus becoming increasingly marked, although it still is much lower then in the United States Congress. A similar pattern of relatively low specialization can be found in many African countries of the Commonwealth, in India, and in New Zeland, with the result that, because of the way in which the United Kingdom has been imitated in this field, Commonwealth countries score lower on committee specialization than the rest of the legislatures.

The reason for this low specialization of United Kingdom committees stems from the suspicion in which committees have been held in the British Parliament, largely because their development was held to have been one of the reasons why the parliamentary system was ineffective in France and why legislation was often bogged down in the United States Congress. It is noticeable that committees have been held under some suspicion in a

---

[3] The number of committees increased from two to twelve in the USSR in the 1960s; the Polish Chamber had seven committees before 1955, nineteen since; the Bulgarian Chamber had four committees to 1958, thirteen in 1970; the Hungarian Chamber experienced a similar increase in committees from four to ten.

number of countries including the United States. The French constitution of 1958 attempted to follow, at least to an extent, the United Kingdom by reducing the number of committees to six, a number which is much smaller than the average for all legislatures and indeed very much smaller than the weighted average for legislatures if size is taken into account. French committees are extremely large as a result, ranging from sixty to 120 members, which is at least twice and up to four times as large as the average for similar legislatures. Even in the United States a reaction against committees developed after World War II, as manifested in various attempts at reducing and streamlining the number of committees in order to make the passage of legislation more efficient than had formerly been the case.[4]

Comparisons between United States and United Kingdom committees can be deceptive, however, and the overall comparison between these two countries and the rest of the world is not truly meaningful unless the functions of the committees and their overall complexity is taken into account. As we noted in Chapter 2, the "proper" function of committees should be to consider matters in detail, both in relation to inputs of legislators (e.g., for new legislation) and in relation to outputs of the executive and the administration. Thus committees should be considered as a means of scrutinizing some of the activities of the bureaucracy and they should have a continuous effect on the development of solutions to problems in areas of policy. In fact, committees of the United States Congress have developed naturally in this direction, in large part because they came quickly to use the technique of the "hearing" in order to investigate the reasons which led to suggestions for new bills. Although United States committees began, in the main, as committees dealing with laws, and although they tended as a result to concentrate in principle on the "traditional" function of legislatures, the scrutiny which they gradually introduced led to the development of a continuous control (or at least supervision) of administrative activities, which in turn led these committees to fulfill to a considerable extent the whole of the functions which committees are apt at fulfilling. In the United Kingdom, on the other hand, the two functions came to be divorced from the start, and different committees were created, largely during and after World War I, to deal with the problem of scrutiny of administration. These committees came to perform this task with considerable effectiveness, through inquiries and hearings resembling in many ways those of the United States committees, but their impact on legislation remained smaller, for the personnel involved in the two activities are not necessarily the same

---

[4] The reorganization of Congressional Committees through the Legislative Reorganization Act of 1946 has not prevented the growth of subcommittees. There were 135 such units in 1968.

and the degree of specialization in matters of administrative scrutiny remained relatively low.

In contrast with these two countries, however, the extent of administrative scrutiny undertaken by committees elsewhere has remained much more limited. Indeed, the legislative committees of the various countries of the world tend to concentrate on legislation and to avoid becoming involved in matters of administration, probably because the technique of the hearing was not developed to any considerable extent, while committees specializing in the scrutiny of administration did not begin to play the part which they play in the United Kingdom. Legislative committees in Latin America and in the Philippines, probably under the influence of the United States, tend to be, on average, somewhat more inclined to scrutinizing the administration than in most Western European countries. Similarly, the newer committees which can be found in Communist countries have been concerned with detailed matters to a greater extent than in Western countries and therefore have been markedly concerned with administration.

The disfavor in which legislative committees have tended to be held in Western European countries is linked to the part which the executive has succeeded in maintaining in the development of the legislative procedure, but it stems also from the fact that in Europe (including France since the 1960s) and in many Commonwealth countries party committees in the chamber have played a sometimes significant part in the preparation of legislation, though not in the control of the administration. Insofar as this is the case (and it might be possible to consider the part played by the Communist party in Eastern communist countries on similar lines), the preparation of legislation sometimes takes place in party committees before the bill is formally presented to the chamber as part of the legislative process. Indeed, in Sweden the part played by royal commissions, on which legislators often sit, constitutes another prelegislature phase which involves some legislators in the discussion and the framing of legislation and which is not different in essence from the type of preparation of bills which occurs in the United States Congress in committees. As we shall see in Chapter 10, these various developments make the analysis of influence on a comparative basis a very complex matter. It follows in particular that the development of policies leading to bills should be considered over a much longer period than is usually suggested. It follows also that the analysis of the extent of discussion in legislative committees of various legislatures constitutes only one of the means of the measurement of the activities of members in committees.

If we do concentrate on these legislative committees, however, we find that marked discrepancies separate legislatures across the world from the point of view of their apparent activities even if the size of the chamber is taken into account. In the first place all members are not members of committees in many chambers, although in the United States Congress all members belong to one, and, in principle, not more than one committee. Moreover, the sittings of committees seem to vary from a low of perhaps a few hours a year (some committees, even legislative committees, do not meet at all in some countries) to a high of hundreds of hours per year in a few countries, particularly in the United States, where each member may spend up to twenty hours per week during the sessions in committee meetings. Given that in the United States committees are especially likely to divide into subcommittees (a tendency which all committees have but which is particularly developed in the United States) the activities of the house as a whole increasingly appear to be dwarfed by those of its committees. Admittedly, this also could be said to be relatively true of many Communist countries (the Soviet Union and Poland in particular), but because the overall level of committee activity is much lower, committees remain very much a part-time affair in these countries, and one which occupies only a fraction of the members.

Yet the development of committee activities everywhere indicates not only that they constitute an important element of the life of legislatures, but also that legislatures are in a process of change which is likely to affect their influence. Possibly because committee activities are more secret than legislative sittings, in that proceedings are rarely published, executives in many countries seem to have come to view committees differently from the way they typically have been viewed by the British government. For this reason the changes which have been proposed in relation to their composition, number, and extent of meetings need to be followed closely, for the problems that crop up may well constitute indicators of the overall role of committees and may also give a more adequate idea of the true nature and extent of the activities of legislatures than the indicators of floor participation to which we now turn.

THE INTERCHANGE BETWEEN LEGISLATORS: DEBATE OR SPECTACLE?

Obviously, the opportunities open to each legislator to participate on the floor of the assembly are very small in all systems. Jamaica and New Zealand give their members four or five hours each year to intervene, and these countries rank exceptionally high. Yet overall averages mask the reality for members of the rank-and-file, as their share of the time is often very small. In the United Kingdon and Australia, for instance, ministers take about half the total time, leaving the rest of the members—five-sixths of the total—only one to one-and-a-quarter hours each instead of the two to two-and-a-half hours on average we listed earlier as the overall average. The situation appears broadly similar in other legislatures, except that in the United States, though not in all presidential countries, ministers have no right to appear and "leading members of the legislature" play the part which ministers may play in nonpresidential systems.[5] Overall, while the relative position of each of the countries remains similar, the absolute amount of time left for debate for each member is about half of what it appears on the overall average.

But this finding is not in itself wholly revealing as it does not suggest the nature of the debate in legislatures across the world. We noted earlier that the amount of time at the disposal of members varied for most countries from one to seven; the fact that back-benchers have less time on average does not suggest that debates are less lively or meaningful in the countries concerned—merely that fewer members speak, and that those who speak concentrate on fewer matters. If we are to assess the extent to which there is true interchange, discussion, or debate, it becomes necessary to examine the activity and the tone of the activity of legislatures in somewhat more detail. For this purpose two indicators can be used which give at least an impression of the extent to which members participate and of the temperature of this participation.

The first is the percentage of members of the assemblies who speak at any time during a session. Clearly, if this percentage is very small, either the assembly is essentially run by the government or by a few supporters of the government, or there is an inner elite which is probably involved in most of the decision making. Unfortunately, the data gathered in this survey were too scattered to permit exact comparision over a range of countries, but they do at least seem to suggest that legislatures tend to be scattered fairly evenly over a "participation" continuum. Broadly speaking, countries divide into three groups. In the first, where participation is highest, about a quarter of the members or even fewer do not participate at all. Atlantic countries are in this group, as is India. Latin American countries seem to show an even higher degree of participation, with only 9 percent of the Uruguayan legislators not participating at all. In the middle group—Madagascar and Singapore are examples—a number of legislatures appear to give the opportunity to speak to about two-thirds of their members. Finally, at the very bottom, only a tiny fraction of the legislators had an opportunity to intervene in East Germany and the Soviet Union; only thirty-five of the 430 East German legislators spoke in the course of the 1970 sessions, and none of them spoke more than once.[6]

In the next chapter we shall examine some of the characteristics of the type of interventions of members of legislative assemblies, but here we are

---

[5] In some Latin American presidential systems, ministers appear and defend their policy on the floor. This is very frequent in Chile in particular, where "interpellation" debates develop as a result.

[6] See Appendix II.

concerned with determining the nature of the debate. In this regard we should note that the situation in two of the three Communist states which are analyzed here (in Yugoslavia, on the contrary, nearly half the members of the Council of Nationalities spoke during the nine sittings which took place in November 1969) shows that "debates" in Communist assemblies have a very different character from debates in all other countries which have been examined—a fact which reinforces the conclusion which was drawn from the analysis of the number and duration of sittings. Indeed, detailed examination of these debates shows marked differences. In East Germany, for example, the sitting of the popular chamber consists of a series of speeches by a number of representatives of each of the groups in the chamber, which include not only the various political parties which form the coalitation but also a number of social and economic groupings such as the "Kulturbund," the "Freie Deutsche Jugend," and the Women's organization.

This contrasts with the situation in all other chambers, including those which meet very infrequently, such as Singapore. There the debate is not restricted to any representative, for the back-bencher does speak and makes points, either on the details of bills or on bills in general (as well as through questions). Interestingly, Madagascar and Singapore are both countries in which the number of meetings is small and the average amount of time per legislator is the smallest; these are also two of the countries in which the percentage of members who remain "speechless" or inactive throughout the whole session is the largest. But it is also interesting to note that this difference is smaller than the difference in the amount of time which each member has on average at his disposal, thus indicating that, as with bills, there is a tendency for speeches to be shorter, and more informal, where the size of the chamber is relatively small. Indeed, when the debates of these small chambers—particularly that of Singapore—are contrasted to those of the larger chambers which exist in most of Western Europe as well as in Chile or Venezuela, it appears that an "inflation" of speeches takes place as the audience becomes larger. This might account for the fact that the percentage of nonparticipants is lowest in a small chamber which meets fairly frequently, such as that of Uruguay. Overall, chambers meeting relatively infrequently seem to show a slight tendency to have a larger proportion of passive members, but the lack of frequency of meetings seems compensated for, in the smaller chambers, by the shortness of the speeches. The really large contrast is between Communist chambers and others: only in Communist chambers is the legislature essentially composed, at least apparently, of "spectators" who come to hear their leaders.

The number of divisions constitutes another indicator of the activities of legislatures. In the United Kingdom, for instance, the number of divisions per year is very large—over three hundred, or about two per sitting on average. This figure contrasts with the situation which characterizes most countries, although the analysis here is made difficult by the fact that, in large parts of the Third World and particularly in Latin America, votes either are not recorded or are recorded only occasionally. Figures in Appendix II, therefore, are only indicative of the general trend, although they do show the range of the variations, thus making it possible to refine somewhat the participation index, particularly between legislatures which meet frequently and legislatures which meet less frequently.

If most countries outside the Communist area are more or less uniform in giving their members broad opportunities to speak, differences are much sharper on divisions. Atlantic countries (except New Zealand) and Latin American countries (except Venezuela) show a high to very high daily division average; indeed, the Latin American legislatures studied appear even to have a larger number of divisions than those of European and other Atlantic countries. Single-party system legislatures show a much lower ratio of daily divisions, which are in fact very rare in some of these countries, particularly those where the legislatures meet very infrequently, such as Singapore, Madagascar, and Senegal. But divisions do take place, and they are not necessarily on party lines, given that those countries have one-party or near one-party systems, whereas the Communist countries studied, except Yugoslavia, do not appear even to have any divisions.

From this preliminary examination of public activities, it seems possible to distinguish between three types of legislatures. First, Communist states (except Yugoslavia, but probably including Poland and Rumania) display essentially symbolic characteristics. Rank-and-file legislators do not participate, or participate very little, on the floor; meetings are infrequent and are not occasions for debates. However, one should not infer from the limited amount of public activities in Communist chambers that they do not perform any of the functions which we considered earlier. We shall have to come back to this point in later Chapters. But the fact is that debates do not take place. Public meetings are occasions or gatherings which may or may not be conducive to a sense of greater support among both members and the population at large. These are the only legislatures which have these characteristics, although the situation is probably somewhat similar in Guinea.

Another group of legislatures, mainly in one-party African states, though probably in one-party states or near one-party states elsewhere, displays different characteristics from those of Communist states. Here the debate is real and the meetings, though relatively infrequent, are occasions for members to participate in fairly large numbers. The public activities of these legislatures are essentially confined to lawmaking, however, and the laws which are passed concern relatively unimportant matters, or at least matters which affect the social and economic development of the country only to a limited extent. These laws give occasions for discussions, but, possibly because these states are one-party states and often have a charismatic leadership, voting occurs very infrequently.

Finally, legislatures in the Atlantic and Latin American states as well as in many Commonwealth states (in fact, a disproportionately large number in relation to their socioeconomic development) tend to meet much more frequently and to display all the characteristics which are normally associated with legislatures—that is, voting is frequent and participation is high. Members may not have a much greater opportunity to participate in each bill than in the legislatures of the previous group, largely because more bills are passed and also because members seem to speak longer—to make speeches—particularly when the chamber is large. (It will be recalled from our discussion in Chapter 5 that the ratio of members to the population is higher in these states.) But these chambers also are involved in other activities alongside lawmaking, often to a very marked extent. (France and Switzerland are exceptions to this generalization, being, for different reasons, more similar in this respect to legislatures of the previous group.) Overall, European and North American legislatures do not display characteristics which are markedly different from those of many Commonwealth legislatures and several Latin American legislatures, and the fact that Atlantic legislatures meet more frequently seems in large part attributable to their larger size.

Thus the legislatures of the contemporary world may not be "powerful" according to a theory of legislature supremacy, but the large majority of them are at least "meaningful." The public activities are not a sham, except in the Communist states. Only for Communist states (except Yugoslavia) is it really necessary to introduce a different model and to give a different meaning, at least to floor activities. Given that we know that the role of legislatures in lawmaking is likely to be limited by executive influence, however, it becomes necessary to explore the various aspects of legislative involvement, starting with the legislators themselves.

THE
LEGISLATORS
7

Legislatures are institutions that fulfill a number of functions. They are also bodies of men and women with aspirations about their own careers and the future of society which stem in large part from their own backgrounds as well as from the environment. Naturally enough, the achievements of a particular legislature will depend on the extent to which legislators can be said to be "motivated" as well as on the constraints which are imposed upon the institution; and the direction and means of these achievements will be guided in part by the "socialization" process through which the members of the legislature come to choose the career in which they are engaged.

The study of legislators, therefore, is not only part of the study of the process of elite-formation, but is also an important part of the study of the nature and character of legislatures. Yet the problem is complicated by one major difficulty of a theoretical kind: we know that, *in some way*, the backgrounds, career aspirations, and ideologies, as well as the personality characteristic of legislators will affect the nature of the process by which legislatures come to influence decision making. But we lack a precise theory of the *extent* to which such individual factors will affect this process. Moreover, because the "folkways" of legislatures tend to mold the personnel, individual characteristics of legislators may be modified appreciably by the institutional fabric, making the cause-effect relationship between legislators and legislatures reciprocal. Constraints imposed by governments on legislatures become "internalized"; members of long standing know what is "possible" and indeed may exaggerate difficulties, passing on this information or these attitudes to new members who may not, as a result, be as aggressive or as articulate about their aspirations as they might otherwise have been. In other words, the requirements of a career may work against the ideological predispositions which the members may have brought with them into the legislature.

At least until an acceptable theory of the relationship between "attitudes" (and background) and behavior has been developed, both in general and in relation specifically to legislatures, we need to be very careful about attempting to extrapolate from the characteristics of members to those of legislatures. This pitfall has not altogether been avoided in the study of attitudes and background of legislators in a number of countries. Up until recently, there has been a tendency in studies of legislatures to concentrate on the men rather than on the collective outcomes of the actions of these men, possibly in part because of the difficulties of data gathering, but more probably in order to apply to legislators the same techniques as those which had been applied quite successfully to mass electorates. But mass electorates are, on balance, only involved in *one* political action, that of voting, whereas legislators are involved in a large number of political activities. They know each other well and interact in many ways. Legislators thus form groups, or, as has sometimes been suggested with reference to the British House of Commons or the United States Senate, "clubs." The behavior of legislators, therefore, cannot be easily deduced from the study of attitudes, and even the notion of "role" constitutes only a partial means of explaining behavior.[1]

THE SOCIAL BACKGROUND OF LEGISLATURES

THE UNREPRESENTATIVE CHARACTER OF LEGISLATORS

From the point of view of a photographic image of the social groups in countries of the contemporary world, legislatures are unrepresentative and the only question which arises is how vast is the distortion between the composition of the country and the composition of its legislature. Although adequate data can be obtained only for about a third of the legislatures, the spread of the countries is such that there is no possible disagreement with the overall finding.[2] Distortion exists with respect to the four indicators of the social composition of legislatures which can be used—age, sex, education, and occupational background.

1. *Age* It is natural that legislators should be older than the "average" citizen of a country, so that it is least to be ex-

---

[1] The attitudes of American legislators (principally on the state level) have been studied carefully in the 1960s. Cf. J. C. Wahlke *et al.*, *The Legislative System* (New York: John Wiley & Sons, Inc., 1962); and J. D. Barber, *The Lawmakers* (New Haven: Yale University Press, 1965).

[2] See Appendix III.

pected that on this indicator legislators will provide a representative cross-section. The average age of legislators hovers between forty and fifty, with European and North American legislators tending to be around the upper limit and Communist legislators not being appreciably younger. This is natural since life expectancy and therefore the average age of the population is higher in the Western world and in the Communist world than in the Third World in general. In the Third World, however, the average age of legislators tends to be located at both extremes, with Latin American and Asian legislators apparently being as old as or older than legislators in the Atlantic world while legislators in other parts of the Third World are younger—sometimes much younger. Thus in Africa, for instance in Ghana, Zambia, Cameroon, and even more in Chad, the average age of legislators is forty or less. The newness of the political system may account for this situation, although the turnover of legislators is not appreciably higher in these countries than it is in some countries of the Third World where the average age is higher—for instance, India. Clearly, the traditional nature of the political system in some parts the Third World (as Colombia or Jordan, for example) accounts in part for the fact that the legislatures of these countries comprise a large number of old men.

2. *Sex*   Sex leads to one of the largest distortions in the representative process. With women in a majority in the world as a whole and in each country, they are nowhere in a majority in legislatures and usually constitute a tiny minority of members. On this issue countries fall into three groups. In the largest group, women are an almost insignificant proportion of the total. Whether in Atlantic countries or in the Third World, percentages vary usually between 1 and 2 percent; in some cases, possibly by accident, the percentage rises to 5 and 6 percent (Colombia, Equatorial Guinea, India). Social pressures and career inhibitions operate, both in developing and developed countries, to a very marked extent to produce this situation.

In a few countries the proportion of women is higher, reaching either 10 to 15 or even 30 percent. In the first of these two groups, three types of countries can be found: the Scandinavian countries, most Communist countries, and Guinea. In the second of these two groups, one finds, at least in the sample analyzed here, only East Germany and the Soviet Union. Clearly, the condition of women in Scandinavia and a determined effort in the Communist states have made for the difference. Yet even in these two groups of countries the percentages of women remain low relative to the population as a whole.

Interestingly, even though, as we shall see, some countries have introduced "quotas" for various occupational groups, they have not done so in relation to women outside the Communist bloc. (Guinea is the only Third

World example, together with, at a much lower level, Equatorial Guinea and India, where social or political pressures probably have been exercised to select women for the legislature.) Moreover, not only do women play a minute role in the legislatures of Atlantic States outside Scandinavia, but their number has not increased since World War II. Thus these political systems not only do not "naturally" produce a sizable representation of women, but they are not even likely to allow for better representation in the future if conditions remain the same.

3. *Occupations and education*   The occupational and educational background of legislators can be examined together since they are closely correlated. On both counts legislatures are markedly unrepresentative. Industrial workers and agricultural workers or farmers generally are greatly underrepresented, as are persons with primary education only. Conversely, different groups of professional men, businessmen, and what might be called "party career men" are overrepresented—sometimes markedly so—as are men with a university education.

An analysis of the extent of under- or overrepresentation of various groups must take into account the occupational and educational breakdown of the countries concerned. For purposes of simplification, it is perhaps admissible to divide the world into four groups of countries on the basis of their level of economic and educational development. In the first group (mainly Atlantic countries) 10 percent or less of the population is engaged in agriculture, between a third and two-fifths are in manual industrial employment, and the rest divides between a small proportion in business, management, and the professions and a much larger proportion in clerical occupations. In a second group (mainly Communist countries) the proportion of the population engaged in manual industrial occupations is about the same or only slightly smaller, but the agricultural population is larger. The third group consists of countries which are at an intermediate level of economic development (such as Turkey and many Latin American polities) and which employ about half to two-thirds of their population in agriculture, a small percentage in industry, and the rest in business and clerical occupations. Finally, in a fourth group of countries the overwhelming majority of the population is engaged in agriculture and the industrial sector is very small: this group is composed of most of Africa, large parts of Asia, and some Latin American countries.[3]

The agricultural population is underrepresented in all groups, but particularly so in the fourth. In a few developing countries the percentage of legislators with a background in agriculture reaches about a quarter or a third, but this is only a third of the ratio of agriculturalists in the population

[3] See Appendix III.

at large. In Communist countries and Atlantic countries, on the other hand, agricultural underrepresentation usually is not so marked, the percentage of agriculturalists in the legislature being as much as half the figure for the population at large. In a few cases—New Zealand, Norway, and the United Kingdom—farmers are actually not underrepresented at all.

Workers also are underrepresented overall, even in the Communist states. The extent of underrepresentation is greater in Atlantic states than in Communist states, however, even where Social Democratic and Communist parties are strong. This distortion is of course greater where these parties do not exist or are very weak (United States, Canada) or happen to have obtained few seats in the legislature (France). Elsewhere in Western countries, workers constitute about 10 percent of the legislature, in contrast to 20 to 25 percent in Communist legislatures. Among Communist states East Germany and Yugoslavia are extreme cases, with workers constituting 44 percent of the chamber in the former and only 1 percent in the latter. Of course, in countries of the fourth group the percentage of workers in the population is so small that this underrepresentation is of little significance in these cases. In some Third World polities (notably the United Arab Republic) they even are overrepresented, but this is both deliberate and exceptional.

Professional men, including teachers, businessmen, managers (mainly in Communist countries), professional politicians, and especially lawyers are overrepresented. Lawyers form a sixth to a fifth of the legislators of most Atlantic countries, even though they are an insignificant proportion of the total population. In North America they form the majority of the legislatures, and this is also the case in many Latin American countries, in the Philippines, and in some more "traditional" countries of the Third World. No other occupation is so overrepresented, and in so many countries. Business and management as well as teaching usually also have a greater share of the seats in the legislatures than their numbers in the country would warrant, whereas clerical workers are typically underrepresented, at least in industrial countries of both West and East. Moreover, persons with a high level of education tend to constitute the majority of legislatures everywhere, but nowhere in the world are they in a majority.

Overall, distortions tend to be sharp everywhere. They tend to be sharpest in the Third World, but this is because of population changes in Western countries rather than because of changes in the legislature, for as the percentage of the population engaged in agriculture declines, and as the percentage of manual workers also begins to decrease, legislatures become an increasingly unrepresentative cross-section of the country as a whole. This is in many ways a natural consequence of the seemingly unavoidable constraint which education places on legislatures. The job of legislator requires some education if it is to be fulfilled adequately; indeed, the more the chamber is active and influential, the more it is important that at least a large proportion of the members be able to understand problems of administration and some of the highly technical questions linked to administration. Lawyers, managers, and professional people are therefore at a premium, irrespective of the social advantages which they have and of the freedom to stand and participate in legislative work which their jobs give them. Some "natural" forces are therefore at play here, although political beliefs, to which we are now coming, also have tended to play a role in fostering biases in representation.

THE THREE "STAGES" OR TYPES OF REPRESENTATION

Educated men of middle age dominate most legislatures, but the variations which we noticed also suggest that other social groups are of importance. It seems possible to note the existence of three distinct types of representation toward which political systems tend to gravitate. The first could be described as the "lawyers' paradise" it cuts across both the Western industrialized world (especially North America) and the Third World (Latin America in particular, but in a number of other countries as well). The second model is that of Communist states, where "workers, peasants, and the intelligentsia" are represented in large proportions, with the latter, consisting of party officials as well as managers, markedly overrepresented. In the third model, which seems to be emerging in some parts of the developing world, civil servants, teachers, and managers appear to play by far the most important part. Although many countries, notably many Atlantic countries as well as developing polities, are characterized by a "mixed" situation, it is interesting to consider these models, and even to see them as successive phases through which some countries have tended to go or may be going.

The model of the "lawyers' paradise" can be said to have been the first form of modern representation, when the main problem was to ensure that individuals or relatively small groups—interest groups—had a voice in the machinery of government. It is the first form of modern representation, either because it came about when the legislature was created or because it replaced the model of landlord domination which was not in a true sense representation. Lawyers played an important part in the development of modern legislatures because of their general representative function in courts, as well as because of their professional skills, their ability to intervene in debates, and their knowledge of the laws.

The "lawyers' paradise" model was challenged, however, when the notion of working-class representation began to acquire momentum in Western Europe. The idea was to open up legislatures first to the common man, and increasingly to manual workers, who were viewed as being both oppressed and underrepresented. This was especially important insofar as the oppression was held to be the result of the underrepresentation. Socialist and Labor parties regarded winning representation for their clienteles as an important part of their program before World War I. This idea was naturally taken over in the Soviet Union and, later, in other Communist states. But, alongside the ideology of working-class representation *per se,* stands the more general notion of representation of social groups, or at least of those social groups which the state recognizes, an idea which manifests itself in Western Europe in coalition systems and in Eastern Europe (East Germany, Poland) and in some of the "forced coalitions" often found there. When this theory of representation is applied to the whole of the legislature, the assembly becomes no longer a place where spokesmen *for* groups congregate (as in the case of the lawyers' paradise), but a place where true emanations *from* these groups come to express their views and those of their peers. Behind this theory, presumably, is the assumption that it is not possible to trust others to speak on behalf of these groups.

It is in this light that the notion of representation of interests, which plays an important part in Western European legislatures, should be understood and examined. On balance, American legislators represent interests somewhat more indirectly than Western European legislators, whose interests are often determined by their background. Trade unionists are often held, and sometimes expected, to represent the interests of their trade union; business "representatives" and "representatives" of a variety of interest groups are also fairly common in the legislatures of Western countries. Although the analysis of the links between legislators and various interests may be misleading because it might assume exaggerated influence, it is indicative of a type of representation which stands halfway between the "brokerage" idea and the representation of sections of the population.

Indeed, European countries have probably always been genuinely ambivalent about the two forms of representation, since there are parallels between the Communist notion of representation and the representation of estates as it took place in medieval Europe. The composition of European legislatures, therefore, should be understood on the basis of a threefold distinction. First, a tradition of "estate representation" leads to the representation of various groups in most political parties, including right-wing and center parties, as one can find in particular in Christian Democratic parties in many countries of the Continent. (See Table 7–1.)

Second, the idea of "brokerage" and "juridical representation" as epitomized by lawyers emerged and might have prevailed by the nineteenth century had it not been for the appearance of a third form of representation championed by Socialist and later Communist parties. These parties emphasized and attempted to implement the notion of representation of workers

Table 7-1.   Occupational Background of Members of Christian Democratic
Parties in European Assemblies (percentage)

	Date	(1) Profes- sionals	(2) Business	(3) Managers	(4) White Collar	(5) Farmers	(6) Workers
Austria	1968	7	20	7	34	25	5
Belgium	1965	33	20	–	40	5	0
West Germany	1953	18	13	2	25	13	21
Italy	1958	⁻36	3	12	39	4	0.4

Source: Austria: A. Pelinka and M. Welan, Demokratie und Verfassung in Österreich
(Vienna: Europa Verlag, 1971).   Belgium: F. Debuyst, La fonction parlementaire en
Belgique (Brussels: CRISP, 1967).   W. Germany: W. Hirsch Weber and K. Schütz,
Wähler und Gewählte (Berlin: Franz Vahlen Verlag, 1957).   Italy: J. P. Chassénaud,
Le Parti Démocrate chrétien en Italie (Paris: A. Colin, 1965).

and of the intelligentsia—and to some extent farmers and some agricultural
workers, though these often had more successful "peasant" parties to
represent them. This is why an analysis of the composition of Socialist and
Communist parties in Western European legislatures shows marked re-
semblances between these parties and legislatures in Eastern Europe. In
practically all the countries of Western Europe, a monopoly or near
monopoly of working-class representation belongs to Socialist and Communist parties, although this is less true where Christian Democratic parties
are strong. Nevertheless, these Socialist and Communist parties are not
overwhelmingly composed of workers; even Communist parties do not have
a majority of workers in their parliamentary groups. Overall, the different
traditions have led to a combination of the two models in Western European
countries, and this combination does not appear to be any less stable than
the "purer" models which exist in America or in the Communist countries.
    Indeed, it could be argued that the Communist model of representation

Table 7-2.   Occupational Background of Members of Communist Parties in
the French, Italian, and Soviet Legislatures (percentages)

	Profes- sional	Business	Managers	Teachers	White Collar	Farmers	Workers
France (1962)	4	0	3	22	17	10	44
Italy (1958)	13	1	44	8	10	–	24
Soviet Union (1966)	–	–	34		16	19	27

Source: P. Ferrari and H. Maish, Les groups communistes aux assemblees parlementaires
(Paris: PUF, 1969).   M. Lesage, Les régimes politiques de l'URSS et de l'Europe de
l'Est (Paris: Presses Universitaires de France, 1970).

of "peasants, workers, and intelligentsia" is itself a halfway house, as it represents a compromise between the normal, "static" idea of "representation" of social groups such as workers or peasants (and intellectuals in the narrow sense) and the more "dynamic" notion of representation embodied in the Communist party's conception of a "vanguard" of the proletariat. Party activists and managers are represented—and indeed overrepresented—in the Communist legislatures not merely because they are an intelligentsia, but because they are the means by which the state operates and develops: they are the "engines" of the whole system. If one pushes the idea further, one can see that a more extreme model would be one which attempts to ensure that the monopoly of representation in the legislature is in the hands of those groups which constitute "the hopes of tomorrow."

In fact, however, no country seems to have pushed the conception to its extreme conclusion, but the representation given to managers, civil servants, and even the military in some of the Third World states does seem to suggest that these countries attempt to implement, at least partially, such a conception of representation, which indeed is not a "representation" in the normal sense, but a translation in the present arrangements of the legislature of the ideals which the state has for the future. It is understandable that this should be the case, inasmuch as developing countries do not have (or at least do not claim to have) "classes" in the sense that industrial countries have; the point, therefore, is to develop the nation and to see that new ideas become accepted, while new elites are made to implement these goals. In such a situation, lawyers would simply maintain the old system and landlords would do so even more staunchly; manual workers are too few to constitute a solid base for representation; the bulk of the population living on the land is too poor and too ill educated to constitute the basis for the legislature (although in the UAR, an effort is being made in this direction). Thus the legislature should be composed of men of the "new class" rather than of landlords, lawyers, workers, or peasants. Curiously enough, this theory corresponds to actual practice only in Yugoslavia among Communist states; in different ways, it seems to be developing in some Third World States, such as the UAR, Cameroon, and Tunisia. In the Eastern Communist countries, at least in the developed Eastern Communist countries, it is unlikely to become the norm, both because of the industrialization of these states and the role which the "working class" plays in the ideology and also because representation in the classic sense is likely to become increasingly more important as these countries become more affluent. Conversely, the "representation" of the new technological and managerial classes is likely to increase in many Third World legislatures and it is indeed likely to give to these legislatures characteristics which are very different from those of more traditional assemblies.

THE CAREERS AND
EXPECTATIONS OF
LEGISLATORS

HOW MUCH OF A CAREER IS THE LEGISLATIVE CAREER?

It seems to be generally assumed that to become a legislator is to take up a career. This assumption probably stems from the widely held belief in the importance of the legislature as a decision-making body. Yet the rapid turnover in many Western countries suggests that the matter needs to be carefully considered.

The turnover of legislators across the world shows very marked variations, from a high of 100 percent in some countries to a low of about 15 percent in the United States, with a fairly even spread in between.[4] Broadly speaking, below some Latin American countries (such as Costa Rica) where the figure is 100 percent because legislators cannot stand immediately for reelection, the turnover is as high as two-thirds in some African countries, the Soviet Union, and India. A further group of countries, scattered across the world shows a turnover of about 50 percent, while most Western European countries are located at the low end of the continuum, with turnover rates of between 20 and 30 percent. Thus the legislatures of Western liberal democracies appear to be characterized by an exceptionally low turnover compared to the rest of the world; but the fact that the turnover in India is as high as it is in Kenya or in the Soviet Union suggests that turnover is not necessarily linked to the type of political system.

There are institutional or near-institutional reasons for some of the very high turnovers. In some countries, mainly in Latin America, the constitution states that legislators cannot be candidates immediately for reelection. The rule was probably first introduced during the French Revolution and was applied, albeit with some rather unfortunate effects, for the election of the French Legislative Assembly of 1791. There are more flexible versions of this rule, which are designed to prevent legislators from staying in office for more than a short period. Yugoslavia has introduced requirements that limit the term of office of all office-holders, including legislators but not including President Tito. Other countries—in particular Communist countries—attempt to introduce *in fact* some form of rotation in order to ensure that a "class" of legislators will not be created and that some men will not become entrenched in their positions and powerful as a result. This type of arrangement also can be found in a number of new countries. In the Ivory

[4] See Appendix III.

Coast, for instance, the increase in the size of the legislature which took place in 1971 coincided with an effort at "rejuvenating" and thus changing the legislative personnel. Many political systems tend to break legislative careers in order to avoid creating a "political class." Membership in the legislature is thus of necessity only one of several careers for a given individual in the course of a long private and public life.

However, the attempt made in many new countries or new regimes to shorten the length of the legislative career coincides with the fact that, in other countries, the legislative career still remains short, apparently through natural attrition and under no institutional pressure. Even in the Latin American countries in which there is no legal provision imposing a break in the legislative career, the majority of legislators remain in office for the period of a term or at most two terms. The situation is similar in India. Indeed, the same also occurred in the past in many liberal democracies of Europe and North America. In the United States, for example, the turnover of congressmen was very high in the early period of the Republic.[5] It also was very high in Canada at the end of the nineteenth century and in Switzerland up to World War I. It may be that the leaders of new countries who attempt to reduce the length of the legislative career by legal fiat or by political pressure simply fight an unnecessary battle and that short tenure, though not of course 100 percent turnover, would occur naturally even if no constraint were imposed in these new countries.

What the history of the legislatures of Atlantic states suggests, however, is that turnover tends to decrease over the very long period, and it has done so for all those countries for which data were available for a long period. We can trace the gradual decrease in the turnover in the American Congress in the nineteenth and twentieth centuries. Although the situation in 1800 was not very different from what it is now in the Soviet Union or India, by the late nineteenth century the situation resembled the current situation in Chile, and by the 1950s and 1960s the percentage turnover was the lowest of all the countries. Similarly, the percentage of new entrants in the Canadian Parliament or the Swiss National Council has decreased gradually over the last fifty years. And, if the turnover in Chile in the 1960s resembled that of the United States in the second half of the nineteenth century, the turnover in Chile in the 1930s resembled that of the Soviet Union in 1966. In all cases, the long-term trend has been toward a decrease in legislative turnover. This does not mean that the career of the legislator becomes very long: most members, everywhere, stay in the legislature for

---

[5] N. W. Polsby, "The Institutionalization of the U.S. House of Representatives," *American Political Science Review*, LXII (1968), 144–68; A. Kornberg, "Parliament in Canadian Society," in A. Kornberg and L. D. Musolf, eds., *Legislatures in Development Perspective* (Durham, N.C.: Duke University Press, 1970), p. 123.

Table 7-3.   Percentage of New Members in Various Legislatures over Time

	USA	Canada	Switzerland	Chile (Senate)	Colombia
ca. 1800	50				
1850s	50				
1890s	35	50			
1920			44		86
1925-35				67	
1930s	20	45			
1935					76
1944			38		
1940s		38			
1950s-1960s	10-19	20-25	28	41	66

Source: U.S.:   N. W. Polsby, "The Institutionalization of the U.S. House of Representatives," American Political Science Review, LXII (1968), 144-68. Canada: N. Ward, The Canadian House of Commons (Toronto: University of Toronto Press, 1963).   Switzerland: E. Gruner, L'Assemblée fédérale suisse, (Berne: Franche, 1970).   Chile: W. H. Agor, "The Senate in the Chilean Political System," in A. Kornbeig and L. D. Musolf, eds., Legislatures in Developmental Perspective (Durham, N.C.: Duke University Press, 1970), pp. 228-72.   Colombia: J. L. Payne, Patterns of Conflict in Colombia (New Haven: Yale University Press, 1968).

only ten to fifteen years, not more. If the group of new entrants decreases, it is mainly the "mid-tenure" men who benefit. The legislative career is therefore at best a "career in the making" in most countries, and a short career elsewhere. The expectations of legislators about their future and their vision of their role surely depends to a considerable extent on the changes taking place in this career as well as on the build-up of the legislature as an institution.

THE EXPECTATIONS OF LEGISLATORS AND THEIR VISION OF THEIR ROLE

Given these large variations in the career potential over time and space, and given also the variations in opportunities of legislators in different types of political systems, a comparative study of expectations of legislators would probably reveal major variations. Yet, at this stage, the study of attitudes of legislators toward their job has only begun and it has taken place in a small number of countries only. As a result, the typologies of legislators which have been constructed have tended to be restricted so that few inferences can be drawn from them.

Among American congressmen and, to an even greater extent among state legislators in the United States it is possible to distinguish between various "types" which have been given labels, such as the "tribune" (speaking for the people), the "ritualist" (doing the work as the rules suggest), the "inventor" (trying out new ideas of bills), the "broker," and the "opportunist."[6] It has been found that the large majority of congressmen divide fairly evenly between the first two roles. Moreover, when asked about the way in which they see their relation to the electorate, American congressmen find themselves mainly in a position (described as "politico") which is intermediate between that of a Burkean "trustee" and that of a "delegate" of the constituency.

However useful, these typologies may be as a first mapping of views of legislators—and, indeed, as a source of possible comparisons across legislatures—they do not reveal much about the intensity with which these feelings are held and the types of consequences which follow from them. Presumably, they apply also, for instance, to members of the Supreme Soviet, who, as we shall see in the next chapter, have to take into account the views of constituents and can even be recalled.[7] What is therefore critical is to be able to appreciate the extent to which these feelings are held and the general "regard" in which the function of legislator is held by the members.

Such a distinction—based on interest and willingness to return—between various types of legislators has indeed been put forward by J. D. Barber, but it has hitherto not been applied to legislators generally, nor indeed to legislators in the United States.[8] Barber's study of Connecticut legislators suggests that there is a sizable percentage (18 percent) of legislators in that state who are only very "reluctantly" involved, and that two further categories (which he labels "spectators" and "advertisers") do not correspond to the mythical ideal of the "lawmaker." Indeed, this ideal type of the legislator, who is both active and interested, constitutes only a minority (34 percent). One would expect the percentage to be higher in the American Congress, in view of the low turnover rate which we have mentioned already and which suggests that the United States Congress is one of the most sought after legislatures and one in which the notion of a career is best established.

Two studies, one of Belgium and the other of Colombia, show that the correlation between intensity of interest in the job and turnover rates may well be high. Belgian parliamentarians seem generally somewhat disaffected

---

[6] R. H. Davidson, "Congress in the American Political System," in Kornberg and Musolf, *op. cit.*, pp. 161 ff. Among primary roles, United States Representatives split into 47 percent "tribune," 41 percent "ritualist," 7 percent "inventor," 4 percent "broker," and 1 percent "opportunist."

[7] Ten deputies were recalled between 1958 and 1966, and one was recalled in 1968. M. Lesage, *Les régimes politiques de l'URSS et de l'Europe de l'Est* (Paris: Presses Univ. de France, 1970), pp. 317–18.

[8] Barber, *op. cit.*, p. 20.

about their capabilities and their efficacy. There are more parliamentarians who believe in their efficacy at the local and regional level than at the national level; what is more, only a small minority believe that such a thing as a legislative "career" exists, while the majority is either frankly negative or mildly negative about the profession and its opportunities.[9] The case is even stronger in Colombia, where, as we saw, turnover is very high, largely because "getting re-elected is generally an exhausting task and demands considerable motivation."[10] The job is defined as boring and dull. Overall, it does seem, from these as well as many impressionistic accounts, that the motivation of legislators is probably appreciably lower than is normally idealistically expected, partly because the expectations in many cases were very high before entering the legislature and the confrontation with the reality was somewhat traumatic, partly because of the nature of the constraints imposed on legislators, the structure of the leadership within the assembly, and the general conditions of work.

Clearly, one of the inhibiting factors in the motivation of all members is the part played by a few in the "management" of the legislature. Senior members of the American Congress control the committee chairmanships and thereby much of the flow of business in both houses. The same is true of influential British MPs—former ministers, for example—and Privy Councillors often have been accused of monopolizing, or at least dominating, the time on the floor—that is, the time not taken by the ministers and the front benchers of the opposition. We noted in the preceding chapter that, in the East German popular chamber, only representatives of the parties and groups had in fact participated on the floor of the assembly during the whole of 1970. This situation, which is extreme, finds itself reproduced in a milder form in most of the legislatures of the contemporary world. Ministers, rapporteurs of committees, and leaders of parliamentary groups all have much more of a say in the deliberations of legislatures than "ordinary" legislators. Moreover, because leaders of parties very often control who will speak on behalf of the party in key legislative or other debates, they in fact control indirectly the degree of rank-and-file involvement in a very large majority of the speeches which take place on the floor.

In all the countries for which an analysis has been undertaken, it emerges that the top 10 percent of the members of the legislature tend to occupy between a quarter and a third of the time on the floor; this percentage can be found in chambers which are as different and varied as the French National Assembly, the Swiss National Council, the Malagasy

[9] F. Deboyst, *La Fonction parlementaire en Belgique* (Brussels: CRISP, 1967), pp. 320–23 and 369–54. J. L. Payne, *Patterns of Conflict in Colombia* (New Haven: Yale University Press, 1968), pp. 238–67.

[10] J. L. Payne, *op. cit.*, p. 241.

Assembly, and the Singapore House. Different indicators suggest that the top 10 to 15 percent of the Canadian House of Commons were the only members who were truly involved very markedly in the activities of that assembly,[11] while an examination of questions in the Indian parliament also shows that less than 10 percent of members are responsible for about half the questions. At the other end, near the group of legislators who do not participate at all on the floor and who constitute at least about a quarter of the legislature, is another sixth or fifth who seem to play a very little role—as for instance in France, where they were responsible for less than 7 percent of the interventions and in Switzerland for about 8 percent. Clearly, these members are not truly concerned with what happens in the legislature, at least in general. Whatever the constraints placed upon them, and irrespective of the fact that, in some cases, activities in committee or behind the scenes may compensate to some extent for limitations in overt activities, they constitute a large group of "spectators" or of "reluctants," whose apathy can be explained only in part by the influence of the government, of the committee chairmen, of the rapporteurs, and of the leaders of parliamentary groups. Their motivation to be in the legislature probably would be increased only marginally if greater powers were given to them.

If low motivation and leadership "domination" combine to reduce the motivation of many members, the conditions under which they must operate are another factor often cited by members themselves to account in part for the relative dejection in which many find themselves. In a broad sense, the matter is closely related to the "model" of the legislature which prevails in a given country as the conditions under which legislators are able to operate are linked to an ethos of professionalization which either clashes or coincides with the accepted views on representation. Where the legislator is deemed to be a "representative" in the juridical sense implied in the "lawyers' paradise" model, there will be a tendency to give him the means by which he can act as a "professional." He will have a salary which is consistent with that of a full-time manager or executive; he will receive assistance from permanent officials of the legislature in order to undertake the research which he feels he needs to do; he will have access to information which is required for that research; and he will have means of publicizing his actions in order to achieve redress. Where, on the other hand, the legislator is considered to be a delegate from a given section of the population, he will tend to be viewed as a part-timer who goes to meetings of the assembly mainly in his spare time, just as a delegate from a trade union or any other organization goes to conventions or congresses without losing touch with the constituents with whom he daily mixes. Because he is

[11] Kornberg, "Parliament in Canadian Society," in Kornberg and Musolf, *op. cit.*, p. 99.

viewed as a part-timer, access, publicity, and information, as well as professional staffs, usually will be denied him, for his purpose is more to express views which stem from the grass-roots than to explore problems "submitted" by constituents.

Thus one can rank legislatures along a broad continuum which places at one end assemblies such as the United States Congress and other highly professional bodies, and, at the other, the Supreme Soviet of the Soviet Union and the legislatures of other Communist states. In Western European countries the notion of the part-timer is still widely adhered to. When, as in Switzerland, the assembly meets for short periods, however intensive, the requirements of a permanent professional staff, of a large pay, or of general facilities become less important by contrast with the need to make sure that the assembly work does not prevent members from being active in other walks of life. The motivations and expectations of legislators become markedly changed as a result.

It is therefore very important to consider the general conditions under which the legislature operates in order to understand the attitudes of legislators and their relation to the "career" which they have embraced. This is clearly why, on a comparative basis, feelings of intensity in relation to the functions which have to be fulfilled should be examined very carefully and placed within the context of the outcomes and the modes of behavior which characterize these assemblies. Clearly, in the contemporary world, the increase in the complexity of government has led many legislators to ask for greater facilities in many advanced industrial countries, and in particular in Western Europe, where, as we saw, the conception of the legislator has tended to remain ambivalent because of the complex nature of representation in these countries. Indeed, the gradual increase in professionalization of legislators in Western countries probably will find itself repeated outside of the Western European area, as is already apparent in parts of Latin America. The vision which legislators have of their role will be modified as a result and this is likely to affect, to some extent, the collective behavior of the legislative bodies and therefore their effect on outcomes. It is thus important to bear in mind the role and character of legislators when considering these outcomes and the influence which the legislature may have in delaying, changing, or speeding them up. Whether we consider detailed actions at the individual level (to which we now turn) or intermediate and general activities (which we shall consider in following chapters), the origins and relative newness of legislators as well as the prevailing views about representation will clearly have a part to play.

LEGISLATORS AS AGENTS OF DETAILED CHANGE

8

In order to measure the influence of legislators, we know that we must try to compare the part which they play at the most detailed level with the more "exalted" role played at the level of policies, whether intermediate or broad. For a variety of reasons, action at the most detailed level is likely to appear unimportant; policy is not at stake, little of what is done in this area contributes to the ostensible prestige of legislators. Yet these detailed activities are among the oldest undertaken by legislators and it is probably true that many legislatures—at least those with the longest history—owe their existence and role to the desires of some constituents to have a body capable of enacting highly limited policies affecting only few of them. The taxation and lawmaking powers of assemblies were, in the American colonies, in France, and even in Britain, due in large part to the desires of a few constituents to see their basic demands met by the government or to prevent the government from encroaching on what they felt was their preserve or their area of autonomy.

We need, therefore, to try to assess the roles which legislators play in meeting such demands and in assisting in seeing grievances redressed. We also need to see, as far as possible, how often these roles occur in various types of polities. In these matters, as we indicated in Chapter 2, informal action is very common, so that description and measurement are perhaps even less effective than at other levels. Nevertheless, an impression can be obtained both of the extent of activity and of the extent to which this activity leads to elements of change. To do so, we need first to describe the types of demands and grievances with which legislators are confronted and the volume of grievances which tend to come their way. We will then have to consider the means by which they come to know the demands and the way in which they pass on, and press for, these grievances. Only thus will we be able to consider, at least in general and in different systems, whether they are successful in being agents for the people in their day-to-day problems and, if so, to what extent.

THE DEMANDS OF CONSTITUENTS: THEIR SCOPE, EXTENT, AND PROCEDURE

WHAT DEMANDS?

The definition of "detailed demands" by constituents is somewhat arbitrary. They can cover questions that concern a specific individual for a particular period (why didn't he obtain a particular grant? or is he entitled to some benefit?) as well as questions which might concern a relatively large number of persons in a constituency, such as the provision of road improvements or the extension of a school. Clearly, these matters involve inputs and outputs; as we noted in Chapter 2, the distinction between inputs and outputs is not conceptually clear-cut. For example, constituents may be concerned with pressing a matter as a new demand and may suggest some new approach to the administration because they have been turned down at a prior period with a request relating to changes about an output of the administration which concerned them.

One conclusion which emerges clearly from the accounts of pressures on legislators for detailed matters is that the subjects usually cover a whole variety of matters which concern only very indirectly, if at all, the government and the administration of the country. Legislators are being asked to intervene in questions relating to local government or to public corporations which have, in many countries at least, an independent status vis-à-vis the government. They are sometimes even made to consider family problems or private matters relating to parent-children or husband-wife relationships. This is because the functions of the legislator in this context effectively are those of an arbitrator or of a "tribune" of the people, both more influential and somewhat impartial. Thus the least influential constituents, those who are afraid to go to social workers or government offices, will tend to approach legislators for a variety of grievances and demands which could, and indeed eventually probably will, go to the "regular channels."

THE ORIGINATORS OF DEMANDS

Detailed demands emerge, as we have just seen, both from individuals who have a limited knowledge of the workings of the administration and are uneasy about procedures as well as from groups of individuals and associations who are concerned specifically with a problem of administration, typically with a local or sectional twist. Evidence for this variety of origins is scattered across the world, but it appears to extend to all types of political systems, though probably not to the same extent. In Tanzania and in the Soviet Union, as well as in Britain and the United States, originators of demands seem to vary across virtually the entire possible range in terms of their interest in politics and their sense of their political efficacy.[1] But associational demands are better documented and probably are more numerous where the average level of education is higher; by the same token, literacy also affects the ways in which demands are communicated to legislators.

THE CHANNELS OF DEMAND-MAKING AND THE VOLUME OF DEMANDS

Everywhere, demands are communicated both through informal contacts with legislators and through mail, but it seems that mail plays a greater part in the demand-making process in Western countries than in either Eastern or Third World countries. For the countries for which some information is available, it appears that legislators tend usually to hold forms of "surgeries" during which they meet constituents at regular intervals. The more the assembly meets, the more this type of activity has to be regularized and tends to take place on specific dates (usually weekends) and in predetermined places. These are the occasions when "ordinary" men tend to pass on their grievances to legislators; and these tend to be the occasions where the grievances conveyed are mostly concerned with matters of a personal kind which may not deal with the central administration and indeed may not deal with administration at all.[2]

At the other extreme, informal meetings with legislators in the chamber itself are more likely to be triggered by individuals or associations which have an administrative grievance, and may even lead to group demonstrations if the assembly meets frequently. There are no reports, for instance, of such activities involving deputies to the Supreme Soviet, and in general it is unlikely that they should take place frequently in political systems which

---

[1] For Tanzania, see R. F. Hopkins, "The Role of the MP in Tanzania," *American Political Science Review*, LXIV (1970), 754–71. For the USSR, see P. H. Juviler, "Functions of a Deputy to the USSR Supreme Soviet," unpublished Ph.D. dissertation, Columbia University, 1960.

[2] This is true in the Soviet Union (see Juviler, *op. cit.*, pp. 134 ff.) and the United Kingdom (cf. R. E. Dowse, "The MP and his surgery," *Political Studies* (October 1963), pp. 332-41.

do not allow or allow with considerable reluctance the involvement of citizens in public demonstrations relating to their grievances.

Between these two extremes, the volume of mail received by legislators is probably the most sensitive indicator of the extent to which constituents are involved actively in an effort to see their grievances redressed by legislators and of the extent to which they believe that legislators are likely to be successful in redressing these grievances. Of course, the extent of mail is also related to the literacy level of the country, which in turn is related to its degree of socioeconomic development. In Western liberal democracies the matter has been studied to some extent, and it is clear that, in many cases, mail is so large that it can constitute a serious bottleneck, unless considerable assistance is given to legislators—particularly to those who both hold positions in the government and are members of the assembly. In the United Kingdom it seems that, on average, MPs receive between twelve and twenty letters a day, many of which cover matters extending much beyond individual grievances.[3] In the United States, congressmen seem to receive about five times this amount of correspondence—a figure which, interestingly, corresponds to about the amount in the United Kingdom, if it is recalled that the number of British MPs per constituent is about five times larger than it is in the United States (435 Representatives for over 200 million, as against 630 MPs for about 52 million). About 12 percent of this volume of mail represents individual demands, with another 15 percent emanating from constituents on a wider variety of issues.[4] These two countries probably constitute the maximums at present reached by legislators' mail. Emphasis on matters other than mail at any rate unquestionably plays a greater part in the descriptions of the demands made on members of assemblies in other parts of the world.

THE MEANS OF CHANNELING DETAILED DEMANDS

As we noted in many instances, the structures or procedures by which legislators handle problems (or fulfill their functions) vary considerably across the countries and are indeed varied within each legislature. If we leave aside those problems which concern certain constituents privately, are not related to a public agency, and are handled by the legislator directly, the means of channeling demands extend from informal and "unofficial" activities, which are carried out everywhere to a varying degree, to official activities which also exist everywhere, but differ in kind as well as in extent.

---

[3] P. G. Richards, *Honourable Members* (London: Faber & Faber, Ltd., 1959), p. 167.

[4] D. G. Tacheron and M. K. Udell, *The Job of the Congressman* (Indianapolis: The Bobbs-Merrill Company, 1966), p. 282.

In all the legislatures about which some information is available (and there is no reason to believe that this is not true of other legislatures), informal activities relating to detailed demands are extensive and repeated. At the lowest level, legislators serve as intermediaries between constituents and the bodies which are able to process the request. These bodies may not be governmental; they include particular local administrations and other decentralized public authorities. The legislators' activities in this area include the pressing of already made claims as well as the channeling to the proper authorities of claims which had not been well directed. At a higher level, informal activities include discussions with government departments and with ministers, by correspondence and by personal visits, of matters which had been taken up but had provisionally been turned down. Legislators enjoy an access to the central government departments and to members of the government that is unquestionably greater than that of most citizens, even where the chamber meets relatively rarely and the legislator remains essentially a part-timer, as in the Soviet Union and other Communist states. In the United Kingdom, for instance, the treatment of correspondence from MPs is different in form from that which any private citizen will have; but the same happens to the correspondence of members of the Supreme Soviet, who often have opportunities to go to the ministries when they are in Moscow, and who know the appropriate channels.[5]

The more a matter is detailed and personal, the more the legislator will tend to use informal channels and the lower in the administrative and ministerial hierarchy he is likely to go in the first instance. But both because a legislator cannot expect to gain much support for a detailed question from his colleagues unless it is possible for him to argue that the informal channels have been explored and exhausted, and because many detailed matters can be personal in the extreme and therefore gain by not being publicized, informal channels are of considerable importance for a whole variety of issues which would not be taken up at all if such channels did not exist.

FORMAL ACTIVITIES: BILLS, QUESTIONS, DEBATES—PARTICULARLY FINANCIAL DEBATES—AND PARLIAMENTARY COMMISSIONERS

The volume of informal activities relating to detailed matters, whether stemming from constituents or generated by the legislators themselves, is still not well known. Our knowledge of the formal aspects of detailed activities of

[5] Richards, *op. cit.*, p. 169; Juviler, *op. cit.*, p. 145.

legislators is somewhat greater, and the examination of the public activities of legislators suggests considerable variation in volume and in techniques. Even though we assume that detailed (and in particular highly personal) questions are dealt with by informal techniques, it is nevertheless the case that problems of a detailed kind tend also to be handled by five types of more formal arrangements, two of which are particularly useful for matters which are somewhat personal while the other three are more appropriate for matters of a somewhat impersonal, perhaps local or sectional, character.

1. The first two of these techniques do not involve activity in the assembly itself, but are nonetheless "formalized" in that they force the governmental and administrative machinery to act, at least to the point of investigation. One technique, the written question, is very common. It is particularly used in Western countries to handle detailed matters (and specifically constituency matters), although letters to ministers probably achieve almost exactly the same aims where the technique does not exist in this form, as in the United States. The informal character of such questions, and the fact that they do not lead to a debate in the assembly and thus are not heard by others, means that they are more likely to be used for detailed matters than most other techniques.

Up until recently, the written question and/or semi-official letter was the most common means by which pressure could be put on detailed questions. The development of parliamentary commissioners in a number of Western countries in the course of the 1960s suggests a further and more formal step. This technique was created in Sweden, spread to various other Scandinavian countries, and extended to the United Kingdom, Commonwealth countries, and indeed to some parts of the continent (Germany) in the 1950s and 1960s. In the United Kingdom the parliamentary commissioner is triggered by the action of an MP who decides that there seems to him to be a prima facie case of complaint against the administration, but it is the parliamentary commissioner who carries the procedure further and who reports to the House as to whether the matter does indeed suggest the existence of a case of maladministration.[6]

The ombudsman has spread to only a minority of countries, however, even though the spread has been fairly rapid. Where it does exist, informal methods of handling problems are also to some extent parallel by actions in the courts, and in particular administrative courts, and other types of inquiries which constitute substitutes for parliamentary action. In a number

---

[6] See W. Gellhorn, Ombudsmen and Others (Cambridge: Harvard University Press, 1967), in which nine countries are covered (Denmark, Finland, New Zealand, Norway, Sweden, Yugoslavia, Poland, the Soviet Union, and Japan). For the United Kingdom, see G. Marshall, "Parliament and the Ombudsman," in A. H. Hanson and B. Crick, eds., The Commons in Transition (New York: Fontana, 1970).

of cases, the development of these inquiries stemmed from the action of legislators, though the case has to be such that the matter can be raised either in committee or in the assembly as a whole, thereby creating such a stir that the assembly itself starts an inquiry or the government had to give way and appoint a committee to inquire. American Congressional committees and subcommittees sometimes may be involved in this way, and various assemblies have in fact induced governments to undertake such inquiries, as was the case in the United Kingdom with the Crichel Down affair.[7]

2. The other three techniques are public and involve the use of the "time" of the house on the floor. They are therefore used more sparingly for detailed matters and more commonly for problems which are less detailed or at least less personal than the problems amenable to the techniques previously analyzed. One of them, that of the presentation and passage of bills, relates typically to inputs; the other two, oral questions and small debates on the one hand and the listing of grievances during financial debates on the other, concern both output control and the preparation of inputs.

In a small minority of legislatures, detailed questions are passed to the decision-making process through the use of large numbers of *bills.* These may be either plain private or local bills or bills which, under the guise of generality, concern in fact specific matters. It is in the United States Congress that this technique is most commonly used, though this is in part because, for historical reasons, many matters (such as the granting of decorations) are done through the technique of a bill where, elsewhere, the executive would be empowerd to act.[8]

Apart from such truly private and detailed legislation, members of assemblies sometimes become involved in attempting to press on the legislature some bills which remain detailed in scope and very limited in their effects. This is only the case, however, in very few assemblies and the extent of use of the technique, even where it takes place, is very limited.[9] In Western Europe, in most of the Third World, and even more in Eastern Europe, private members' legislation has a limited scope which is even smaller for purely detailed matters. But for limited and detailed problems, the introduction of bills, as well as their discussion, may be of as much importance as their passage. By presenting a bill relating to a detailed issue,

---

[7] The Crichel Down Affair resulted from administrative malpractice in the United Kingdom Ministry of Agriculture and led to the downfall of the minister. See R. Douglas Brown, *The Battle of Crichel Down* (London: The Bodley Head, 1955).

[8] Almost six thousand bills were introduced in the House of Representatives in 1968, for instance, the large majority of which were "private" bills.

[9] It is used to a fairly large extent in Uruguay and Costa Rica, though not on the scale found in the United States.

the member of an assembly can act in the same way as other members act by presenting written questions or writing officially to ministers. The question is publicized and the process of gradual involvement of the government or other colleagues in the matter starts being operative.

On the whole, however, detailed questions tend to refer to problems which regulations or other acts of the executive typically should deal with. Thus the two other techniques—those of the *question* or small debate and of the *financial debate*—play a much greater and much more widespread part. Questions, as we saw, exist in the Commonwealth and many other countries, particularly if we include in this category those very short debates in which one or two members "talk" to a minister. Many countries outside the Commonwealth do not use the technique at all, or only very rarely.[10] Moreover, most oral questions and most of the short debates tend to relate to general matters of administration. In the United Kingdom Parliament, for instance, only a minority of questions can be said to be concerned with truly detailed matters. But questions can be used in this way and are indeed sometimes so used, mainly where the detailed matter can be expected to interest more than a few members and thus raise problems of principle or indicate administrative obstinacy to which members could be expected to react.[11]

Thus, by some curious accidental and quasi-universal development, debates on finance have tended to constitute one of the main means by which members raise formally, on a yearly basis, some of the detailed questions which affect their constituency or some of their constituents. This is true in the United Kingdom and in the Soviet Union, in France and in Madagascar, though it is of course true only where the discussion of the budget takes place on a reasonably broad scale. Almost certainly, such detailed questions are also but forward and discussed in the privacy of committees, despite the fact that this bypasses the opportunity to use the full house to publize ideas and to show constituency concern. More perhaps than through questions or debates on bills, debates during budget sessions constitute the expected form by which ministers can be "hooked" to problems which they might otherwise have thrown aside or left in abeyance. Thus the role of these debates as a safety valve in the overall channeling of detailed questions is of major importance, although on this, too, a systematic analysis probably would reveal varieties in the patterns and help to define with precision the level of the questions raised. On the whole, it seems that economic matters relating to constituencies and local problems touching individuals or small groups tend to be aired and examined. Even though

[10] See Chapter 6.

[11] See D. N. Chester, *Questions in Parliament* (London: Oxford University Press, 1962), pp. 184–87.

outputs are being controlled and the administration checked in this way, such debates do not address themselves to problems of clear-cut maladministration as is normally the case with questions sent to an ombudsman. They also do raise new questions, and in this sense they constitute in a true fashion the equivalents of private bills introduced or discussed to cover specific matters: they are designed to lead to new regulations or orders as well as to check the work of ministries.

THE EFFECTIVENESS OF LEGISLATORS IN CHANNELING DETAILED DEMANDS

Because so much is done in private, because ministers often reply evasively to questions or points made in financial debates, even though they may in the long run take account of what has been stated, it remains difficult to have more than general impressions about the actual effects of the various procedures we have been discussing. But it seems admissible to suggest three broad points in connection with detailed demands.

The first is that legislators consider that it is their duty to be involved in these matters and that detailed questions, however trivial and, indeed, however far outside the scope of governmental powers, need to be considered and pursued. Admittedly, there are considerable variations in the degree of interest of legislators for local matters. In Western countries the contrast is usually drawn between "constituency" members and members concerned with broad policy matters, but few legislators—including ministers —can afford to forget completely the life of their constituents. In Eastern countries, and in particular in the Soviet Union, members of the party apparatus seem much more concerned with broad policy questions. The members who deal with constituency questions tend to be, on the whole, workers or "peasants" who live among fellow workers and are more aware of detailed grievances, though members coming from the civil service seem also to be concerned with problems of detailed maladjustment and may even be more apt at dealing with the matter.[12]

On the whole, there seems to be much concern with detailed matters which, probably in most cases informally but in many cases formally as well, lead to the legislators' action. Indeed, in the last resort detailed activities relate to the overall machinery of administration; occasionally they may raise major issues and end up raising broad political issues. Even where legislators cannot achieve broad or even intermediate-level policy change through one law or other broad legal documents, they may hope to achieve the same result, over time, by stressing detailed difficulties.

[12] See Juviler, *op. cit.*, p. 153.

Secondly, the problem is almost the converse for the executive. However inconvenient it might be for some civil servants, and even for ministers, to be subjected privately to the lobbying of members and to be subjected to complaints about detailed issues, governments can channel criticism and reduce it to levels which are politically innocuous. It has been noted that, in the United Kingdom, where discipline is strong it is on detailed matters that MPs of the government party can most easily make their grievances felt and thus express an amount of criticism which members of legislatures probably feel is their duty to express. In the Soviet Union, criticisms in the implementation of economic and even social policies at the most detailed level are the means by which it is possible to give to the legislature some appearance of liveliness and to give legislators a truly effective function. It may be that, in the long run, a whole series of detailed criticisms can undermine the executive or at least bring about some change which goes beyond the detailed level at which it has been pitched. But, for the executive, the safety valve constituted by detailed criticisms is one which is likely to be closed only in the most extreme authoritarian cases.

Thirdly, and because of the two points just raised, it seems that detailed activities probably have some effectiveness. They are effective in the first place, by the very fact that they exist. Because constituents can talk to their legislators in the United Kingdom or Madagascar, in the United States or in the Soviet Union, the tension which might otherwise exist is by itself somewhat relieved. Similarly, because the legislator can be involved in this way in matters of a detailed kind, because he can approach ministers and civil servants, and because he can also, almost everywhere, make his colleagues note the problems and confront ministers publicly, additional effectiveness is achieved. In the second place, it is undeniable, from at least partial evidence from a variety of countries, that actions of legislators contribute to changing situations and redressing difficulties. Where, as in the United Kingdom and in other countries which have an ombudsman, the grievances passed on for examination can be listed and checked, one can indeed note and measure the extent of effectiveness in dealing with maladministration. But even where no ombudsman exists, accounts of successes in a variety of public matters have been given, whether for the United Kingdom or for the Soviet Union, for the United States or for Germany. And, finally, it is inconceivable that legislators should be, as they are, involved in informal actions at the local and central levels if they did not, from time to time, encounter problems which they solve and where the administration bows. Indeed, if they did not meet with such success, more would be known publicly about the disgruntlements which would ensue.

THE ROLE OF LEGISLATURES ON POLICIES OF INTERMEDIATE IMPORTANCE

9

If we now move along from detailed questions in the direction of general policies, it is convenient to consider problems of intermediate importance, although this notion cannot be precisely defined. Indeed, there are variations. Inasmuch as the distinction is adopted for the convenience of the analysis, the notion remains somewhat vague and covers both matters of some importance which affect only a limited number of people (for instance, the regulation of the activities of a small section of the community) and matters which affect large sections of the population but do not raise acute divisions of opinion and are primarily technical in character (traffic regulations, for instance). Basically, these policies refer to matters on which most sections of the population tend to have no views or only very vague views and about which men with different ideologies can find themselves easily in agreement; disagreements are likely to be due to other causes. It would be an exaggeration to say that these matters are wholly technical, though many of them are; it also would be an exaggeration to say that they develop within the status quo, as any new rule does alter the status quo even if only to an infinitesimal extent. It would be too much to state that these matters are always related to the implementation of principles, though this may well be the case in many circumstances because, in some theoretical fashion, any matter is related to the implementation of some principle. Yet all these points have to be taken into account as they help to determine the halfway point or halfway area between truly detailed questions and general problems.

As we have stated repeatedly, the influence of legislatures relates to the generation of new ideas and to the control of outputs by the administration and the government. Thus, in relation to policies of intermediate importance, we shall need to consider the role which legislatures may have in scrutinizing administration as well as in generating new ideas. Indeed, problems of intermediate importance are perhaps those where one can most easily perceive the dichotomy. With very detailed issues, we noticed that the distinction between new demands and the control of outputs is often blurred. With general matters, which often take the form of bills, the challenge of the legislature usually will take place before the bill is implemented so that the two processes of generation of ideas and legislative reaction will be to some extent intertwined. At the level of intermediate matters, on the contrary, individual legislators are likely to want to intervene by injecting new ideas or raising new problems, while the government and the bureaucracy will be involved, on the other hand, in elaborating rules to cover situations not hitherto dealt with and thus will create controversies in which legislators in turn will be involved.

THE SCOPE AND ORIGINS OF LEGISLATIVE INVOLVEMENT IN INTERMEDIATE POLICIES

INITIATIVES AND RESPONSES

With intermediate policies we need to distinguish between a variety of situations, which are further complicated in practice because of the requirement that legislatures have statutory powers with respect to lawmaking. Legislatures or legislators may be involved in three ways: they may channel demands from the environment at large, they may initiate new ideas, or the executive may suggest new arrangements. In legal terms, however, the problem may or may not imply the passage of a new rule by the legislature. Whether the problem is covered by a statute, a regulation, or another type of executive decision, if the legislature has to pass the instrument, the legislature will tend to be involved in a highly detailed fashion in the specific arrangements, whereas if the new rule does not require formal approval by the legislature, the involvement of the legislature may take much less formal forms. But where the legislature is concerned with an already existing output, legislative involvement arises only from pressures from outside or from the legislature's own initiative, for the executive is unlikely to wish the legislature to control its own outputs.

The scope and types of involvement of legislatures can be reordered in a simpler fashion, however. On the one hand, there are *initiatives,* which relate to new developments; these stem either from the environment acting on the legislature or from within the legislature itself. On the other hand, there are *responses* to executive actions, some of which concern outputs which have not been implemented and may not be implemented legally unless the legislature agrees, some of which may be implemented and are indeed implemented without the legal involvement of the legislature. There are also intermediate positions between these two types of responses, one element of the distinction being the extent of information given to the legislature as well as of opportunity to be involved.[1]

THE ROLE OF OUTSIDERS

Demands and the control of outputs are often triggered by the environment, since both information and outside support are required. This outside pressure typically will come from groups—formal or informal—and not from individuals. The character and strength of the group system are therefore important in determining the nature and the extent of the demands.

Of course, the groups which are involved are not only interest groups; they include firms which happen to be concerned with a particular problem, but they also include "communal" groupings or "social forces," such as tribes or ethnic or religious bodies, which may not have any formal organization and yet have various noninstitutional ways of influencing legislators. This is particularly the case in developing polities. Thus, although the pressure from interest *groups* is largest on the legislatures of countries which are socioeconomically advanced (as can be seen in Western liberal democracies and in particular in the United States), some pressure also will be exercised through other types of groupings.

A second type of problem arises from the way in which groups and groupings are likely to channel these demands. In relation to intermediate-level demands, groups and groupings are likely to put pressure on the executive rather than on legislatures. As these demands are relatively technical and do not appreciably affect the status quo, the group will exercise its pressure on the legislature either because the executive has shown itself to be opposed to the measure or the group has limited access to the executive. This is true in all political systems, even where, as in the United States, involvement of groups with the legislature is very apparent and very large.

THE ROLE OF LEGISLATORS IN GENERATING DEMANDS AND CONTROLLING OUTPUTS FOR MATTERS OF INTERMEDIATE IMPORTANCE

Many actions relating to intermediate-level policies stem from the legislators themselves. Their extent varies, as we shall see, in large part because of

[1] In the United Kingdom, for instance, some types of regulations have to be "laid on the table" of the House. Much of the examination is done by the Committee on Statutory Instruments.

differences in the extent to which procedures are at the disposal of legislators and, consequently, differences in levels of information. Legislators come to their jobs with some ideas and they develop these ideas as they discuss them with other members, whom they try to convince. The links between groups and individual legislators are often very close at this level. Groups will use legislators to push forward some ideas; they will submit the information required on a technical plane. As only a small number of legislators is required for a problem of intermediate importance, groups will hope to succeed even if few members are involved. Consequently, in countries where group activity is low, the degree of specialization of legislators will also be lower and the activities of legislators at the intermediate level probably will suffer; they will tend to be developed only in those fields in which legislators are qualified personally or by training. Thus where the representative principle is based on the notion of the "lawyer's paradise" and where the groups are well articulated (which is the situation in the United States), any type of intermediate policy is likely to be presented. On the other hand, where the principle of representation is based on various social groups, and where interest groups are less well articulated, as in the Soviet Union, demands expressed and outputs controlled at the intermediate level are likely to be restricted to a fairly narrow range of problems.

MEANS OF ACTION
IN RELATION TO
INTERMEDIATE POLICIES

THE ACQUISITION OF INFORMATION AND THE ROLE OF COMMITTEES

As we saw, legislators exert pressure in regard to matters of an intermediate kind if they themselves, or groups behind them, suggest ideas. But their response to executive action depends largely on acquiring information about this action. Thus, in systems which are more open, which have better communication media, and where legislators have better assistance of a collective or individual character (e.g., libraries or assistants), they will be better informed. But other factors also come into play here, such as the size of the country and the level of development of the bureaucratic machine.

Legislative committees play an important part in this process. We noted in Chapter 6 that committees are often concerned with the scrutiny of administrative outputs, in connection with and as an appendage to lawmaking, in connection with the passage of budgetary and other financial matters, or even in some cases as a wholly separate type of activity. To the extent that these committees concern themselves with matters other than laws, they will obtain a greater amount of information about intermediate-level outputs of the administration, which they will in turn be in a position to control. Inasmuch as committees which extend their activities specifically to these matters exist only in a small number of countries—most notably in the United States, fairly recently in the United Kingdom, and to a more limited extent, in some other Western European liberal democracies—it follows that in other countries the information obtained in relation to inter-mediate-level outputs of the executive will be small and essentially limited to bills. In this case, opportunities for effective control will be insufficient.

One reason why committees are particularly well adapted to informing legislators about outputs of the executive is that the constraint of time which operates on the whole assembly operates much less strongly on the committee system. Nor is there even a constraint on location, as committees can trans-port themselves almost wherever they wish. Thus the development of sub-committees of main committees and the custom committees may have of making on-the-spot inquiries provide highly effective means of examining the activities of the administration. Nowhere has the use of subcommittees to conduct hearings been more developed than in the United States, though in other liberal democracies it has begun to be customary, in the 1960s at least, almost certainly under the influence of the United States, for com-mittees to go and investigate on-the-spot the activities of the administration. In the United Kingdom and Canada, for instance, special committees of inquiry and scrutinizing committees go and ask selected members of the public and, more usually, members of various administrative bodies about their activities, their goals, and their demands. Elsewhere, the practice is much more occasional, except in some Latin American countries, where it seems to be used mainly when grave incidents have occurred and only rarely in relation to matters of intermediate importance concerning the day-to-day activities of the administration.[2]

PRESSURE, DECISION, AND THE ROLE OF TIME

Before examining the various means by which legislatures, essentially on the floor, come to exercise pressure for matters of intermediate importance, we need to consider those matters in which the legislature responds to initiatives of the executive in advance of implementation, and those cases in which the legislature itself exercises its initiative by passing, or attempting to pass, bills from its own members. In the previous chapter we encountered, though on a very limited scale, a similar problem in connection with detailed matters, where we saw that in some countries, especially the United States, many detailed matters are dealt with by legislation. But the problem reveals

[2] In Venezuela, for instance, a committee was set up in 1969 to investigate grave incidents in the universities.

itself more fully in relation to intermediate matters because it is at this level that matters are sufficiently broad to involve more than a few legislators while being sufficiently technical or nonideological as to avoid leading executives and legislatures into head-on policy clashes.

Strictly, legislatures are involved in *decisions* when they pass or amend bills of governmental origin or when they discuss and pass bills originating with private members. But the process is truly at the border between pressure and decision, inasmuch as the rejection of an amendment or a bill, even at the intermediate level, does not signify that the presentation of the bill or amendment will have no future effect. At one extreme, some bills or amendments might be presented purely for "propaganda" purposes without its supporter or supporters having any hope for seeing the bill through. This is relatively rare in questions of intermediate importance, but we shall see that the method can play a very large part in relation to matters of general concern. Even though the supporter or supporters typically are not so masochistic as to wish to push forward intermediate-level ideas which will not be adopted, a large gray area of problems remains about which members do in fact hope for immediate adoption and about which they are temporarily satisfied if the matter is merely raised. From the point of view of the assembly and even more of the outside world, members are engaged in propaganda and education. From the point of view of the relation between assembly and government, the process is one of *pressure* which may not immediately succeed but which may have some larger or smaller effect in due course. Thus, even in matters of intermediate importance, the question of time is quite relevant, particularly since the action of the executive can be quite widespread and amendments on a particular issue may lead the executive to change either a regulation or simply the "style" in which problems are handled. We therefore should consider the adoption of amendments or the passing of private members' legislation as merely an extreme form of pressure being applied on the executive, either by way of initiative or as a response to outputs.

THE MEANS OF EXERTING PRESSURE

To some extent, pressure is exercised on the executive in matters of intermediate importance through a variety of informal activities, but these play a more limited part than in relation to detailed matters because the number of persons who need to be involved is larger and the time required to convince these persons informally is necessarily longer. To the extent that some legislators have better access to ministers and to the administration, they may be more able to achieve success. In this respect, too, committees are of importance, inasmuch as committees are a means by which contacts are made and access is facilitated. The small size of a country, or of a country's bureaucracy, also increases the impact of these informal contacts. But even at this level informal activities are likely to be one of the ancillary means by which formal developments take place in the decision-making process. Where formal means of exerting pressure are highly developed and widely open to legislators, the influence on intermediate-level decisions is likely to be larger.

In the legislatures of the contemporary world, the means by which pressure can be exerted, either to demand new measures or to attempt to change existing outputs, tend to be of three types which correspond to different levels of formalization and possibly to different rates of speed in the expected outcomes, although of course there is some overlap in both these respects.

1. Some methods of exerting pressure are relatively "vague" and address themselves to a problem, normally without specifically suggesting a solution. These are the debates—ranging from the "question" to the short "interpellation"—which enable legislators to raise "minor" issues. Many legislatures have debates of this kind. In countries of the British Commonwealth which give considerable prominence to question time, many questions are devoted to this type of intermediate issue. In general, however, problems of intermediate importance usually are handled by short debates even though questions can be used in a very flexible manner and can cover the whole range between matters which are extremely detailed and points of general policy. In a number of Latin American countries (particularly Venezuela and Uruguay), as in France since 1958, the short debates which either take place at a given time on certain days or for the whole of some specific sittings cover precisely matters of intermediate importance.[3] In the United Kingdom and older countries of the Commonwealth, however, debates on such matters (usually in the form of adjournment debates and private members' motions) exist alongside questions; these, too, typically raise problems of limited importance which are not controversial in the normal party sense.[4]

Unless a truly political issue is in fact hidden behind the apparent innocuousness of the question, the effect is more to present the problem, to show that there is some concern, and to allow the executive to take note— but, equally, to take little note. Whether a new suggestion is made or an

---

[3] Since 1958, oral "questions" have been introduced in the French Parliament, but they take place only once a week and are in the form of short debates. The same occurs in Venezuela and Uruguay, though the timing of these short debates appears to be more irregular.

[4] The "adjournment debate" which takes place in the United Kingdom at the end of every daily sitting and lasts half an hour resembles in many ways the French "question."

output is being criticized by the member or members involved, the outcome is left for the possibly indefinite future. We begin to see, in this respect, the role of time in the development of ideas. As we shall see in more detail, time plays an even greater part in regard to the most general questions.

2. Two other techniques of exerting pressure are, at least potentially, more direct in their effect, although, as we already noted, the aim may not always be a request for a decision. These are *private members' bills* and *amendments* to government or government-backed bills. Not all private members' bills relate to intermediate-level matters: we saw that some were truly of a detailed character, while others may have a general aim and are likely to be raised, at least in the first instance, for propaganda reasons. The bulk of the individual members' bills for which there is some real hope of success covers intermediate matters while a number of others may even be presented for near-propaganda reasons. Private members' bills have to be used in lieu of questions and debates in some legislatures because these may not be allowed or extensively developed.

Private members' bills are not in use in all legislatures, however, either because they are not adopted or because none are debated or even presented. Amendments are much more common, and indeed almost universal, though committees are typically as important as, or even often more important than activities on the floor with respect to amendments. Like private members' bills, amendments may be raised for the purposes of discussing an issue and they can be withdrawn before being voted on or, indeed, can be defeated without the originator's having hoped to be successful. Amendments also can be raised to air major matters as well as intermediate-level issues, the bill to which they refer being often an indication of the amendment's importance, since an amendment can be as important as the bill but is not likely to be more important unless the amendment is used as a sheer propaganda device. Of all the means which we have hitherto explored, amendments are the technique which is most precisely addressed to a problem, inasmuch as they typically propose a solution to the question under discussion. As a result, amendments are a very sensitive indicator of the strength of legislatures in matters of intermediate importance. The number of amendments *presented* is sometimes as important as the number of amendments passed, just as the number of amendments presented by the executive on its own bills or on bills which it sponsors is indicative of the extent to which the legislature has made the executive alter its position.

3. Finally, as with detailed and individual matters, *budgetary procedure* allows, though in a different fashion, debates on intermediate matters. Although detailed matters tend to be discussed on the floor and usually do not lead to changes in levels of income or of expenditure, the discussion of intermediate questions commonly leads to changes and typically tends to be more effective in committee than on the floor. As with amendments and

private members' bills, changes may be requested without hope of success in order to "educate" the executive and induce it to take the point into consideration in subsequent estimates, but a cursory examination of budgetary practices seems to suggest that this practice is less widely used. Budgetary discussions are probably the most specific and, at least in committee, the most common way in which limited changes in policies take place, whereas bills and, even more, debates and questions are used to raise matters left for future solution.

THE EFFECTIVENESS OF LEGISLATURES IN INTERMEDIATE-LEVEL POLICIES

Legislators everywhere are apt to consider that their importance is slight and that governments generally force them into accepting bills while they are being refused the right to raise matters. But their influence is probably greater than is sometimes assumed and is spread more widely than is customarily suggested.

It is true that debates and questions do not occur in a large number of assemblies (French-speaking Africa, parts of Asia, Eastern Communist States, United States) and that, where they exist, they often occur only rarely and thus do not give to members the opportunity to raise many issues or to make points about administrative outputs (France, many new Commonwealth countries, indeed most continental countries of Europe). (See Table 6–5.) It is even the case that, where the procedure is used to a large extent, its effect is more limited than is sometimes alleged, as for instance in the United Kingdom where it is typically suggested that officials in the ministries worry more about questions than seems warranted, though they do not appear to be much concerned by adjournment debates and by private members' motions. But, as we stated in several instances, matters which give rise to questions and small debates are only occasionally treated as urgent. Members do not normally propose solutions; they make criticisms. To the extent that they air an issue, they may have an impact in the future, though the measurement of such an impact requires much further investigations along lines which we shall discuss at greater length for general problems, for which the question of time has a truly critical impact.

Few private members' bills reach the statute book; indeed, in some countries no private members' bills are passed or even debated. In the United States, on the contrary, the number presented is huge and the number passed, though a minute fraction of those presented, is still quite sizable.[5]

---

[5] Several thousand bills are presented by members of the United States Congress every year. In contrast, British MPs present fewer than one hundred, and so do the members of most Western European legislatures; between ten and twenty of these pass every year. In African legislatures (Kenya, Madagascar, Senegal), private members' bills normally are not discussed, let alone passed. In Communist legislatures, private members' bills are not presented at all.

But even these large numbers should be seen in perspective, for Early Day Motions in the British Parliament fulfill the same function.[6] Moreover, the bills which are passed in the United States are often so limited in scope, as we saw in the preceding chapter, that they count more as detailed and individual measures than as limited policy actions.

Thus one should not consider as truly unique the case of the American Congress, in part because the number of bills presented and passed is markedly inflated for a variety of technical reasons; conversely, the number of bills discussed and passed in many other legislatures is far from being as small as is sometimes alleged. In many Latin American countries, a pattern somewhat similar to that of the United States obtains, not only because particular and individual measures come through the bill procedure (as in Uruguay), but also because the legislature is less constrained to reject private members' measures than is usually alleged. In European countries, too, a number of private members' bills are passed every year. Even though these constitute only about 10 percent of the total legislative output, they do constitute a way for the legislature to deal on its own with some limited questions which probably would not have reached the statute book otherwise.

This situation, therefore, contrasts with that in the legislatures of African and Communist states where private members' bills are unknown or almost unknown.[7] If we take together both the absence of debates (in particular short debates and questions) on the one hand, and the absence of private members' bills on the other, it emerges fairly clearly that, in matters of an intermediate kind, Communist, French-speaking African, and some other African and Asian legislatures are not expected to initiate activities, except perhaps informally. They are not expected either to raise new questions and present new solutions or to make clearly and openly significant recommendations in relation to administrative outputs, at least in ways which would raise the problem in a rather broad manner.

The situation is somewhat different in relation to amendments, though the contrast nonetheless remains between European and Latin American legislatures on the other hand and other legislatures on the other. It is almost uniformly the case that legislatures do make amendments to legislation proposed by the executive, though the form and place in which these amendments are made lead to difficulties of interpretation and suggest the need for a more developed theory of "functional equivalents." On the surface, the United States Congress—and possibly some Latin American legislatures,

---

[6] On the scope and role of Early Day Motions, see S. E. Finer, H. B. Berrington, and D. J. Bartholomew, *Backbench Opinion in the House of Commons* (Long Island City, N.Y.: Pergamon Press, Inc., 1961).

[7] Some legislation emanates from committees of the Supreme Soviet. See P. H. Juviler, "Functions of a Deputy to the USSR Supreme Soviets," unpublished Ph.D. dissertation, Columbia University, 1960, p. 394.

such as those of Chile and Uruguay—are much more prone than any other legislatures to significantly amend laws proposed or backed by the executive. Of course, the amending process which takes place in many other legislatures is far from insignificant, but the bulk of these amendments occurs in committees and are then often "taken over" by the government which presents them as its own when the bill comes on the floor. This is particularly the case in the United Kingdom, where, typically, the government takes over large numbers of amendments presented in committee and, as a form of compromise, both agrees with the amendments and claims them as its own. Indeed, it is precisely at the level of intermediate-level policies that the British executive and many other executives are prepared to accept amendments. An examination of behavior in the French parliament since the Fifth Republic, where the executive is held to be "strong" and insensitive to opposition, shows that alongside a number of private members' bills which French deputies regularly pass, they also pass amendments, sometimes against the government. These are often cast in some compromise form, particularly in matters of limited importance or of a technical nature on which the debate does not raise many major issues. The practice extends to "opposition" parties, including Communists, as well as government parties. Indeed, in the Italian parliament it has been conclusively shown that most of the legislation is amended with Communist help and that the Italian Communist group has therefore contributed significantly in changing, at least at the relatively technical level, the bills which were debated.[8]

Amendments play a much more limited part in other legislatures, even though the give-and-take over legislation of intermediate importance is much more widespread than is often supposed. An examination of the behavior in a number of French-speaking legislatures, in the Tunisian parliament, as well as in a number of new Commonwealth countries suggests that, even though the number of votes on amendments is rare (but not, as we saw, nonexistent), and even though the number of formal amendments passed during a session is also very small, changes do take place on a more informal basis and without the "opposition" or any "group" in the legislature having to force the issue to its extreme formal end. Debates also indicate that some amendments were accepted in the relevant committee, thereby showing that, on technical issues at least, the legislature conducts a "discussion" which, as we noted in Chapter 6, does indeed characterize these legislatures more than is usually claimed.

In Eastern Communist states, except Yugoslavia, however, amendments are not presented on the floor of the house and, indeed, the debate on legislation often has a much more formal and general turn, particularly, as

---

[8] P. Ferrari and H. Maisl, *Les Groupes Communistes aux assemblées parlementaires* (Paris: Presses Universitaires de France, 1969), pp. 48–85.

we saw, in East Germany. However, amendments are also discussed in the committees; indeed, the committee sometimes conducts inquiries on bills it discusses and these are not wholly different from hearings of the United States Congress. The Supreme Soviet was involved in revisions of aspects of the criminal code and of the procedural code for which its committee prepared the work by listening to witnesses and considering, though *in camera*, a variety of arguments. The volume of legislation involved is admittedly much smaller, for the Supreme Soviet is a part-time institution, as are its committees. But those matters which are considered in committee are considered with a degree of seriousness which is not wholly different from that which can be found in other legislatures.[9]

Finally, budgetary discussions give rise, again mainly in committees, to some element of change under pressure from the legislators. This is limited change, amounting perhaps to one percentage point—but we are considering here aspects of detailed policy which could not, in any case, lead to greater changes, for 90 percent of the budget in fact cannot be touched because of regular commitments. On this, too—perhaps even more than on amendments—the influence of legislatures extends far beyond what is sometimes suggested. In all the legislatures for which some record on finance has been obtained (and thus excluding the DDR, Singapore, and Chile—though in the latter case changes are likely to have occurred), modifications have taken place either on the floor of the House or, more frequently, in the relevant committee. Changes are probably greater in the United States Congress, and the procedure by which the Congress handles budgetary matters is also more exacting for the departments concerned. But other executives (including the Soviet executive) also give way, and give way to an extent which is far from trivial, even if plenary sessions suggest that little occurs either in the way of amendments or in financial debates.

The influence of legislatures on policies of intermediate importance is therefore a reality, though this reality seems to be that legislatures normally react, rather than initiate, and that control of truly administrative outputs may be patchy and even rare except in a few countries. Admittedly, the extent of a legislature's influence is not related simply to the strength of the assembly, for executives *allow* legislatures to make changes. In the first place, much more is allowed in committee than is allowed on the floor; almost everywhere, including the Soviet Union, committees are given some power to act independently in matters of intermediate importance. Indeed, committees usually can go further than a mere passive veto; they are involved in change, and to a fairly considerable extent actively involved.

[9] P. H. Juviler, *op. cit.*, pp. 369 ff.

But committees are semi-secret bodies and the tradeoff is that the executive allows for some change if this change remains rather secret.

Secondly, the government often seems prepared to agree to change if the change is somewhat "concealed" and if its prestige can be maintained by the fiction that amendments are its own. Not only the British government, but many other "strong" governments as well (such as the French government since 1958), are prepared to concede amendments provided doing so is viewed as the "gracious act" of a "sovereign agent." Doubtless the characteristics of the modern parliamentary system have led to this situation. Governments have to appear strong and must seem to be leading the legislature; if the appearances are saved, much can be done in fact. Presidential systems, in contrast, do not have the same rules or the same hypocrisy. In the United States or in Chile, the legislature passes laws, provoked or backed by the executive. If amendments are not liked and if the veto fails, as is often the case in Chile, the executive appears to accept a law which it dislikes. In many ways it is this *form*, rather than the substance, which seems to distinguish "strong" parliamentary systems from "weaker" presidential systems. In matters of limited importance, assemblies are not insignificant. But concealment being greater in many parliamentary systems, the outcome in these countries seems quite different from the reality.

Why do governments "concede" this degree of freedom to their legislatures, even in some authoritarian states? And why does this freedom remain within limited bounds? An examination of debates in assemblies shows that, on balance, executives act, consciously or unconsciously, on the basis of some tradeoff arrangements which lead them to agree to some changes in order to secure a general tone of a relatively relaxed debate. Behind this procedure is the need to control the legislature on major issues and the need to maintain in the legislature a modicum of friendship and "good faith." On technical issues, executives do not like to use, and in fact rarely use, major weapons of a constitutional, procedural, let alone coercive kind. As with detailed matters, but on a somewhat higher plane, the need for peaceful arrangements leads to some legislative independence. What is more, the clumsiness of the major weapons makes them, like the atom bomb, somewhat irrelevant to the "little war" problems which intermediate-level questions raise. Moreover, members of legislatures have only a limited interest in, a limited knowledge of, and a limited time for these technical issues. They do not take much positive action because the number of members interested in and competent on each of these matters is usually small and the energy required to mobilize the Chamber to fight the executive or the administration is more than the member can muster, not only because of the strong weapons which the executive might use but because of the difficulties of making colleagues act. The "war" thus remains within bounds: it has characteristics of rearguard actions or of a low-level guerilla. This "war" may be not without influence on the overall outcomes, but it does not go beyond what by some tacit agreement the executive and officials are willing to accept and what the legislators would feel to be a petty and unjustifiable use of executive powers.

THE ROLE OF LEGISLATURES ON BROAD POLICY QUESTIONS

10

The influence of legislatures usually is assessed mainly in relation to broad policies, partly because these are more visible and partly because of their importance. But such an inquiry requires a number of steps. We need first to look at the way in which broad policies emerge and mature and to relate legislatures and the executive to the overall flow of the problems and "ideas" which characterize polities. We then will see how legislatures use a variety of means to attempt to exercise their influence and from this analysis we can conclude under what conditions and for what types of matters legislatures exercise this influence.

THE NATURE AND
SCOPE OF INFLUENCE
ON BROAD POLICIES

CONSTRAINTS ON THE LEGISLATURE AND ON THE
GOVERNMENT—RECURRENT AND NEW POLICIES

It is typically asserted that legislatures have a relatively small influence on general or broad policies, because these are the points at which executives can most easily apply the various types of pressures which they have at their disposal. Party discipline or charismatic leadership will ensure that enough votes will be cast for the executive's position, that the matter will be approved without a vote, or even that it will be approved "enthusiastically" if the case merits. Yet one tends to forget that many constraints operate on the executive itself which reduce its own ability to choose policies. Whether in domestic or in international affairs, the executive's freedom of action may be much smaller than is assumed. It is not correct to assert that the whole of the "power" is in the executive's hands because a legislature makes few "real" decisions in general matters. It may be that the executive had almost no freedom of choice. It may have been constrained by its own bureaucracy to present the measure, because the measure was in effect the consequence of earlier measures or of some inescapable set of circumstances. It may be that the "environment" (public opinion, the world at large, and so forth) effectively has "forced" the executive to act. In such a context, the weakness of the legislature does not automatically imply the strength of the executive. On intermediate matters, it probably is possible to disregard the role of the environment for the freedom of choice of the decision makers is large, but on broad policy issues the amount of change which executive *and* legislature can bring about is typically small, save in very exceptional and temporary periods.

Unfortunately, it is not possible as yet to measure precisely the extent to which constraints operate on executives in regard to general policies. This is particularly unfortunate because the constraints operating on legislatures are perhaps even more visible. But one way of approaching the matter is to consider the extent to which problems tend to be recurrent in a given political system. We noted in the previous chapter, in relation to the budget, that even the Supreme Soviet was far from powerless at the intermediate level, because changes brought about in committees, amounting to perhaps 1 percent of the total budget, constituted perhaps a tenth of the total "possible" change. It must be noted, conversely, that *both* the executive and the legislature are constrained on broader policy choices. Almost everything is fixed inasmuch as nearly all the expenditure has a recurrent character.

Budgets are not the only recurrent policy. If, as we suggested in earlier chapters, we move away from "laws" and "rules" to consider ideas and problems in areas of public life, we see that in many ways recurrence is almost the norm. A comprehensive survey would require examining the rules passed over a long period in a series of polities, but if one takes the United Kingdom as a typical example of Western liberal democracies, one

Table 10-1.   Examples of Recurrence of Bills in the United Kingdom 1961-70
(Financial and other yearly bills excluded;
Scottish and special bills excluded)

Administration of Justice	5	Justices of the Peace	2
Agriculture	3	New Towns	4
Betting and gaming	3	Nurses	3
Civil Aviation	2	Race Relations	2
Criminal Justice	4	Road Traffic	4
Criminal Appeal	3	Rent	3
Education	4	Town & Country Planning	3
Housing	2	Transport	2

sees that transport and road traffic, housing, and education constitute fields of government in which the periodicity of recurrence is short.

The questions listed in Table 10–1 may not all be treated each year or every few years in the same way, but the very regularity with which they recur suggests that events force the problem on the actors, who thus should be seen as groping for solutions rather than imposing them. Moreover, the changes which take place in the context of the problems are likely to be, in many cases, at the intermediate rather than the general level. The impact of legislatures on many of the new rules, therefore, may be fairly large or at least of some moment, inasmuch as legislatures do play a significant part in intermediate-level questions.

The distinction between these "cyclical" and "noncyclical" areas of public policy is perhaps one of the more important distinctions to introduce if we are to assess the role of both legislatures and executives in the development of general policies. Without asserting a linear relationship, we may hypothesize that matters of "cyclical" rule-making are those where events control developments to a significant degree and where constraints on the executive are likely to be quite large, if not necessarily as large as those on the legislature. Where rule-making is not cyclical, constraints on the decision makers are likely to be lower, and if the legislature is to play a part it is in these matters that its role needs most to be assessed.

NEW POLICIES AND THEIR DEVELOPMENT

Without denying that cyclical developments relating to recurrent problems are of no importance in assessing the role of the legislature and of the executive, it is probably easier to perceive this influence in relation to new policies, particularly if we concentrate on matters of a general or broader kind. In relation to new policies, however, the assessment of influence involves taking into account both a positive and a negative aspect, for legislative influence has to be measured both by the type of response which the legislature gives to governmental initiatives and by the way in which its own initiatives are taken up by the government. The problem here is that the government's response is particularly difficult to measure because it raises the conceptual problem of the "nondecision"—namely, the extent to which the government does not present a question, or presents a question but defends it weakly, because of opposition within the assembly. It is not possible to *know*, in the strict sense, although we may have some indication and some clues, what the executive does not do because it does not wish to take up a battle with the legislature which it might be afraid of losing.

Clearly, this area is potentially of considerable importance and we will need to explore it. But in doing so we must realize that our analysis will remain limited, in particular for those countries for which data are difficult to come by and for which, therefore, the background of the "absence" of new problems is not disclosed. As a result, comparisons become extremely difficult. Because the legislature may use different means to stop initiatives of the executive, there is a danger that a legislature will appear stronger where a government "tries" out a law and is defeated than where a government, fearing the consequences and anxious not to appear to be defeated, does not present a new idea. The same problem can arise when we compare different executives within the same country: as we noted in Chapter 3, a "do-nothing" executive would appear "stronger" than an active executive by any indicator which is based merely on the number of defeats of new ideas.

Conversely, the strength of a legislature needs to be measured by the extent to which it tries new ideas and develops them. But, as we have said, such a measurement must recognize that *time* is one of the main factors to be considered in this process. We noted in the previous chapter, in relation to intermediate-level influence, that the distinction between "pressure" or "influence" and "decision" is not clear-cut, inasmuch as the presentation of a bill or an amendment does not necessarily indicate that the legislators involved will consider the rejection of the bill or amendment at one point of time to be the end of the matter. This is *a fortiori* true with general problems. Indeed, it is probably in the nature of suggestions of a general kind that their authors are unlikely to assume that they will be passed at the first presentation. It follows that one indicator of the influence of legislatures in this context is the amount of time needed for an idea to percolate through, rather than a dichotomous distinction between the number of instances in which a suggestion of a general kind stemming from the legislature either becomes or does not become the rule of the country.

The situation is even further complicated by two elements. The first relates to the attitude of the executive. Presumably, since we are considering general ideas, the problem will almost certainly raise an echo within the executive, which will not remain passive in the way it can do on matters of intermediate importance. On general matters, the executive may favor or oppose the new suggestion. Or it may need "educating," in the sense that initially it may not agree to consider a particular problem as urgently requiring a solution. The executive may oppose the proposed move on grounds of "administrative inconvenience" more than on grounds of any principled objection. New ideas—for instance, matters relating to environment and, possibly, civil rights—are often pushed back in this way. Thus a clear distinction must be made between new demands made by the legislature which are opposed to the views of the government and new demands to which the executive is basically "indifferent."

Secondly, it must be remembered that *by definition* the scope of activities of legislatures in relation to general issues will be somewhat limited, simply because (barring very exceptional and transitional periods) the legislature and the executive normally are in accord on the *broad* developments of the country. If they are not, the government will change or the legislature will be in difficulty. It is therefore logically impossible for the chamber to be very powerful and to carry out many initiatives which will succeed very fast in the field of general policies. The organization of the country which would follow from such a policy would be so un-satisfactory that it must be concluded that the scope of influence of an influential legislature will consist of some vetoes or limitations on govern-mental initiatives, some initiatives in new fields hitherto relatively untried, but not a long series of positive victories over the executive.

THE MEANS OF ACTION OF THE LEGISLATURE; THE STAGES OF PRESSURE	The scope of influence of legislatures is conditioned in some way by the extent to which the legislature has juridical and customary means of presenting new ideas and pressing them on the executive as well as of preventing the executive from having its way in all those cases where it initiates either en-tirely new ideas or general policies regarding re-

current problems. On the response side, the action of the legislature depends primarily on its having the means of delaying proposed action by intro-ducing a degree of "viscosity" into the system. On the initiative side, the effectiveness of the legislature will depend on its having the means of making its suggestions repeatedly felt.

"VETO" POWERS IN RESPONSE TO INITIATIVES FROM THE EXECUTIVE

For the reasons which we outlined in the previous section, "veto" responses of legislatures are likely to involve informal means. The public and formal slowing down of the process, therefore, may correspond to only a limited part of the total slowing down. The two main formal means by which a legislature will limit the initiatives of the executive in general matters are general debates (at the limit, "interpellations" and censure motions) and the rejection of government-backed legislation. Where the first of these powers does not exist or is severely restricted, either by the constitution or simply in practice, the "veto" power of the legislature will be much cur-tailed; where bills are not discussed at length or where the government can coerce the legislature into compliance even if they are discussed, this power will be virtually nonexistent. However, delaying tactics will help to increase the behind-the-scenes influence of the legislature more than may be apparent, particularly if the executive is not anxious to be overinvolved in a given new initiative. This is where the general timetable of the legislature has to be considered as a means of effective action, for if the timetable is tight, the strength of the executive may not be sufficient to allow for many governmental initiatives. (The problem here, of course, is that it also may prevent the legislature from developing its own initiatives.) Thus the "veto" power may be quite effective in practice even where it is negligible in theory. The number of meetings of the legislature has a clear effect on the executive and is, therefore, an indicator of its influence in general matters.

INITIATIVES FROM THE LEGISLATURE ITSELF

The situation is somewhat different for those matters which the legislature wishes to initiate as well as on those matters on which the executive can act without the legislature's being much involved. In the latter case, which is likely to occur frequently in foreign affairs or in the field of economic policy, the action of the legislature aims at reversing executive policy. An initiative, however, is necessarily a slow process, whatever means the legislature has at its disposal. It must aim at convincing the executive that there is no alternative but to listen, and be sympathetic to, the suggestion. This will happen if the legislature has means of prodding the executive repeatedly and, at the beginning at least, in such a way as not to antagonize the executive and lead it to use the coercive weapons it has at its disposal. Such a strategy involves different types of means which can be summarized in the following three successive stages.

1. The first stage involves the use of low-key types of pressure. Legislators have to use some of the weapons which we examined in the preceding chapter in a different context. These include the presentation of the problem in the form of short debates, or questions, as well as in the form of bills which the initiator hopes will be discussed. In relation to matters of intermediate importance, the presentation of such bills may be not much more than an effort at counting sympathizers and measuring the intensity of feeling. Bills therefore are presented by a number of members with the intention of obliging the executive, and possibly also public opinion, to take note of the problem. Clearly, where such moves are not open to members of legislature, informal discussion must be substituted, but in this case the legislature is likely to be limited in its effectiveness inasmuch as informal means will not be sufficient for dealing with broad and general questions unless pressure comes from a large number of members. As long as the pressure of members is informal, the executive can in practice discount it. It is, therefore, very unlikely that the second stage will occur unless the idea has come to be aired in the assembly. Short debates thus become a very important way in which assemblies can introduce problems, even though these types of

debates are most commonly used to deal with matters of intermediate importance or of a detailed kind. If a legislature is restricted in the use of these means, its influence will be curtailed on general as well as on intermediate-level problems, and curtailment on general matters will be more important to the executive than on intermediate matters.

2. The second stage aims at forcing the executive to become involved in the new idea by obliging it to examine the matter with some care, unless the assembly itself can do so. With regard to the general problems with which we are concerned here, the investigation will require time and technical support as well as some extensive sounding of views. It follows, therefore, that the required development is toward a formal "inquiry," which might be conducted either by a committee of the assembly or by the executive in response to the legislature's pressure. If the committee system does not make this type of inquiry possible, the legislature must have the means of exerting pressure through debates and questions to obtain an executive inquiry. (Indeed, such executive inquiries may well play important parts even where committees are relatively strong.) If the legislature cannot provoke these executive inquiries, it has to be concluded that the legislature will have little influence in relation to initiatives of a general kind. At best, this influence will be felt only very occasionally, after long periods of time have elapsed—provided that the pressure of the first stage can be repeated frequently so that some movement of opinion gradually takes place in the executive.

3. Thirdly, once the results of the inquiry become known, further pressure will be needed unless by accident the report of the inquiry is entirely favorable and the executive becomes entirely convinced—an unlikely combination of events. If the report is entirely negative, on the other hand, the process will need to be repeated, but this can be done only after a period of time has elapsed. In intermediate situations (which are much more likely to occur), the legislature will succeed only if it can put further pressure on the executive through the discussion of bills and during general and broad debates. This means that success will be achieved only if the assembly has opportunities to initiate such debates and if the weight of other work (due to the executive, for instance) is not used as an excuse for inaction. Clearly, further delays will take place, partly because the executive sooner or later will begin to back or sponsor bills which will be deemed to be unsatisfactory by some in the assembly, and will therefore need to be changed through renewed pressure. Thus the "idea" will begin to be transformed from a "new idea" to one which is "recurrent." But at this stage, as at the previous two, repeated pressure will have to be exercised and the means will have to exist to allow for this pressure. Because these means may not always exist, because changes in personnel may affect the executive and the legislature, and because boredom with the idea may well develop, the

opportunities which the legislature will have to initiate new ideas will be very infrequent at the general level.

What is more, the conditions for the exercise of positive influence are rather different from those which are needed for the satisfactory use of negative or "veto" powers. Indeed, the very factors that enable the legislature to delay governmental ideas also may prevent the legislature from pushing some of its own ideas speedily through the decision machine. Moreover, the effect of coercive and constitutional weapons in the hands of the executive may well be different and somewhat paradoxical. Clearly, if behavioral weapons are strong, the executive will be able to reduce the "viscosity" of the legislature in relation to its own ideas. It also will be in a position to prevent the legislature from developing its own new ideas very far. If, however, the legislature "convinces" the executive of the value of a new idea, the effect may well be that that new idea will be adopted more quickly than where an executive, less able to use behavioral weapons, is frequently stopped by the legislature. A legislature which operates under strong constraints may therefore not be without considerable effect even at the general level.

THE APPARENT INFLUENCE OF CONTEMPORARY LEGISLATURES ON GENERAL IDEAS

"VETO" POWERS, VISCOSITY, AND RELATIVE "IMPOSITION"

In a first approximation, countries which score low on the three indicators which constitute the means by which negative influence can take place are likely to be relatively unable to exercise "veto" powers. If debates are relatively rare, if bills are rarely rejected, and if the overall meeting time is short, it seems reasonable to hypothesize that the executive tends to have its way and that limitations on executive action come from sources other than the legislature. Of course, informal influence may exist and the executive may be restrained from action in a number of occasions. This undoubtedly happens from time to time, but in the absence of data confirming such a state of affairs, we can postulate that the legislatures of the Communist world (except possible Yugoslavia), of most African countries (more so in French-speaking Africa than in Commonwealth countries), and of some parts of Asia (including a Commonwealth country such as Singapore) are not apt to exercise negative influence on general matters. The difficulty comes perhaps more at the other end—namely, in legislatures which score relatively high on at least one of these indicators.

Ostensibly, the United States Congress and the congresses of several presidential countries (Chile, Philippines, and Uruguay in particular) appear to be markedly stronger at "vetoing" executive-backed initiatives. Indeed, it is sometimes the case (for example, in United States, Chile, and Brazil before 1964) that the legislatures of such countries appear much more "conservative" than the executives. In the United States, cases of this phenomenon are well documented and relate to such important issues as education, civil rights, and international trade and cooperation. In contrast, it is suggested that parliamentary executives—in particular those of Western Europe, the older Commonwealth, and India and other parts of the newer Commonwealth—show an ability to get their legislation through much more easily and speedily. This impression in fact may be quite deceptive and the limited amount of evidence which is available, particularly in relation to the United States, the United Kingdom, and some other European countries, shows that the difference may be appreciably smaller.

On the one hand, presidential power in the United States is usually underestimated because calculations are made over a very short period on the basis of a "socialization process" of the country and of the legislature which takes place in the open, with the legislature and its committees being the main forum: the opposition is thus better known than elsewhere. Some of the more general "ideas" of the president take several years or a decade to go through the Congress and a president such as Lyndon Johnson can therefore reap the benefits of the gradual "indoctrination" which took place as a result of John F. Kennedy's interventions, even though the latter may appear very "weak" in relation to the legislature.[1] One should note that the "ideas" of the presidency do tend in the end to go through, and that very few suggestions are indefinitely shelved under congressional pressure.[2] The

---

[1] The *Congressional Quarterly* gives scores of legislative achievement of 48, 45, and 27 percent to Kennedy as against between 48 and 69 percent to Johnson. Although these yearly calculations do suggest some differences, they are misleading in two ways: first, they do not take into account the considerable increase in executive proposals by Kennedy over Eisenhower (from an average of about 225 to 350 a year) and the fact that Congress needed time to become accustomed to such a flow of executive demand; and, second, they do not consider the extent to which time has to pass for ideas to permeate.

[2] The history of medicare, civil rights, and housing legislation in particular show the extent to which, over a period of ten years, the executive eventually succeeds in obtaining its major proposals. The analogous time period in Western European countries is the period of "gestation" of ideas in royal commissions, departmental committees, and so forth, and it would be a mistake to assume that the legislators are not involved during this period. It also can be shown that such committees were of considerable importance in the United States in the 1960s (in relation to crime control and farm labor unions, for example).

executive may not be much less influential in this field than it has proved to be over such crucial matters as the Vietnam war, where the impotence of Congress has been both very marked and very salient because of the intensity of feelings prevailing in this field.

Conversely, the apparent simplicity of the legislative process in the United Kingdon, Sweden, and even post-1958 France masks marked inadequacies of the executive in its ability to control various initiatives. It is not infrequent for the United Kingdom government to have to abandon bills, even of a major kind, because of the apparent reluctance of the legislature to be further involved. In the same way as the President of the United States has a given "capital" of power which enables him to pursue some but not all of his goals, the British Prime Minister may be able to pursue some goals, but only some, if he is intent on presenting new matters to his Parliament. Thus the Labor government of the 1960s was forced to abandon, almost at the last minute, some of its suggestions on constitutional and trade union reform and the Conservatives needed to apply great pressure to steer one important bill, relating to trade unions, during their first year of power after their victory in 1970.[3]

Moreover, the preparation of matters in the prelegislature stage is unquestionably much longer in many Western European parliaments than it is in the presidential systems of North and South America. Trade union and local government reform are only two of a number of instances in which the United Kingdom decision-making process was reduced almost to a standstill because of the apparently necessary prelegislation process which these "new" ideas had to undergo. Indeed, it seems to be the case that the United States government since World War II increasingly has become involved in a similar process. When, in an extreme case such as that of Sweden, royal or presidential commissions start elaborating in considerable detail ideas on legislation and involve many legislators as well as other "interested parties" in the process, it becomes impossible to treat such "new" ideas as being the result of anything like rapid decision-taking and "undue imposition" on reluctant assemblies, for the legislatures are never wholly uninvolved in the preparation stages. "New" ideas are therefore not new and it may be difficult to distinguish legislative viscosity from many characteristics of legislative initiative. The process, obviously, needs much closer examination regarding both the extent of change and the rate of this change.

---

[3] Failures of government bills are more common in the United Kingdom than is usually assumed. They amount to about 10 percent. "Even in the session 1968–69 when the Government ran into so much difficulty, only three of the twenty-four items listed in the Queen's speech failed to become law, and altogether the Government succeeded in enacting fifty-one of the fifty-five bills it introduced." (I. F. Burton and G. Drewry, "Public Legislation. A Survey of the Session 1969–70," *Parliamentary Affairs* [1970], p. 311.) But this means that about 10 percent do fail. Moreover, in 1969–70 the rate of failures increased to 40 percent, although the premature end of the session accounts for this total.

Recurrent problems have become so numerous in Western liberal democracies and in industrial societies generally that the area for new initiatives, both from the executive and from the legislature, may gradually be
reduced. Yet new problems do occur (for instance in the fields of environment and consumer protection) which still leave scope for initiative for
enterprising legislators. Moreover, only a systematic study of the past actions
of legislatures would begin to indicate whether, even in the alleged "golden
age" of legislatures, these actions contributed significantly to the generation of new ideas on broad policy matters.

It appears that the legislatures of a number of countries allow these
long-term initiatives to be successful and that, if the scenario of the three
stages discussed in the previous section can be followed in the legislature, a
number of "one-man ideas" eventually come to fruition. This seems particularly to be the case in the United Kingdom Parliament, where, for
instance, laws on individual freedom (abortion, divorce, and so forth) and
laws on civil rights and race relations can be closely associated with the
activities of a single individual (Lord Brockway) and a very small number
of determined supporters. A similar type of activity takes place in the
United States, where, for instance, aspects of consumer protection legislation can be ascribed to the part played by one individual senator, Paul
Douglas of Illinois.[4] For these one-man actions to be successful, a combination of favorable conditions must obtain—and the time sequence can be
very long, even well over a decade. This makes it imperative or almost
imperative that the persons responsible for the activity both remain members
of the legislature and be characterized by considerable tenaciousness and
single-mindedness. In all cases, the involvement of the executive appears
required at some point, even in the United States. If the idea is of a general
kind and not an intermediate matter, which a short private member's bill or
an amendment could cover, the eventual backing of the executive probably
is required and at least reduces appreciably the length of the operation.

If the sequence is to be shortened, on the other hand, an initiative can
be successful if a bandwagon effect takes place or if the legislature and the
executive both become involved as a result of some outside pressure or
some "new mood" for a new type of policy dealing with a new problem.
Environmental questions seemed to be of this type in the late 1960s in many
Western industrial countries, possibly because of imitation from one country
to another, and possibly out of ulterior political motives on the part of

---

[4] This was also the case with the Colorado River Project, which largely can be
ascribed to the work of Carl Hayden.

executives. In such situations it becomes difficult to distinguish between assembly initiative and executive pressure. Whatever the case may be, if the length of the operation is reduced as a result, the main effect may be to turn the policy area into a "recurrent" problem marked by a series of smaller changes and intermediate actions, even though the problem started as a new idea with a combined action of executive and legislature.

Admittedly, these possibilities of influence exist in only a limited number of legislatures, and, even in the countries where intermediate-level activities are open to the legislature, powers of initiative are often much smaller at the general level. In the Fifth French Republic, some "vetoes" (in the sense mentioned earlier) have taken place and occasional delays have been introduced in the ideas of the executive as the legislature generally has been (in some ways as in Latin American countries) rather more unresponsive to change than the executive tended to be.[5] But the absence of initiatives, in France or other parts of Western Europe as well as in Latin America, does not suggest that the legislature is indefinitely barred from such activities and is consequently constrained to minor influence. In these countries and possibly, though to a more limited extent, in parts of Africa and even in Yugoslavia, the problem is one of gradual acclimatization to a process of influence which requires considerable time to mature, and therefore requires even more time to become accepted as a "normal" process. If an initiative of the legislature in the field of broad policies takes on average at least ten to fifteen years to become the rule for the country, a polity will develop these processes of initiative only if it has experienced "calm" governmental processes for a very long period and if it is not the accepted myth that changes in the government are the ways by which the legislature tends to influence policy. Outside of the Anglo-Saxon democracies and parts of Scandinavia, it is extremely rare for both points to be valid. Either, as in Belgium, the Netherlands, Denmark, Austria, and Italy, it is generally accepted that coalitions can be made and unmade and that patterns of governmental change are, or at least can be expected to appear to be, related to changes in attitudes of the legislators. Thus it could be claimed that these legislators—like French legislators before 1958—have considerable power in making and unmaking governments and, therefore, in seeing that some of their ideas become governmental policy. Or, as in France since 1958, Germany, and many Latin American countries, the "system" has not been maintained for long enough, its principles, myths, and customs have not had sufficient time to establish themselves, and legislators have not developed the

---

[5] The government has at times imposed various forms of pressure in order to avoid "Conservative" backbench revolts; this was particularly true at the time of the Algerian war.

time perspective and the kind of "socialization" which makes it possible for them to believe in the possible long-term effects of "one-man idea."

It is probably true that most legislatures have very little power over broad policies, and that even the few legislatures which have some power in this area play only a relatively small role in the development of ideas. This is because governments, after all, proceed from or at least are generally acceptable to most legislatures. It is also because the number of "recurrent" problems is so vast that, in reality, general ideas in these fields tend to be embedded in technicalities, with the result that new problems and ideas make up only a minority of broader policies. Moreover, it takes time for ideas to mature; because many legislatures are new, because many countries are new, and because myths have not sunk in the habits of legislators, impatience tends to grow and men become diverted from trying out ideas by the short-term satisfactions to be derived from changing governments, changing regimes, or, at the other extreme, leaving the legislature and changing careers. Where there is no legislative career *per se,* as we saw was the case in most new legislatures, and where two-thirds of the legislature is new, initiatives of legislators cannot be expected to succeed; there is little incentive to act and the legislature is therefore more ineffective than it would otherwise have been. It may or may not be a good thing to extend the tenure of most legislators, but it should be clear that their effectiveness in broader policies individually or in groups, with or without executive help, will automatically grow as tenure increases and as the legislature's structure and habits become more recognized. On broader policies, more than on other matters, legislative influence is an acquired taste.

CONCLUSION
THE
FUTURE OF
LEGISLATURES
11

All through this study we have tried to consider legislatures while avoiding two common pitfalls. One is the exaggerated view of the importance of legislatures, manifested by expressions, dating from the eighteenth century, about their "sovereignty" and their full powers in the field of constitution making and lawmaking as well as, in many cases, in government making and unmaking. The other is the overpessimistic reaction, largely due to the idealized and romantic view of the institution, which suggests that legislatures do nothing, that they have "declined," that they are rubber stamps in many countries and increasingly irrelevant in others. Legislatures are neither of these extremes. They are not insignificant, except by comparison with what some people have wanted them to be. They still remain very influential in the countries where they were originally created and they are more influential elsewhere than is usually claimed. From this it would seem that their future is much less bleak than is often supposed—and, indeed, there are reasons to suggest that they are likely to increase and spread their influence, perhaps not so much in the countries where they are at present most important, but in those polities where it is generally felt that their role is minimal or, at best, secondary.

THE OVERALL SIGNIFICANCE OF LEGISLATURES Much of the alleged insignificance of legislatures results from a highly "ideological" line about their role and a lack of examination of their real achievements. Admittedly, we know that there are many reasons why it is difficult to study legislatures: problems of data gathering, conceptualization and language differences, all combine to reduce our apparent ability to draw true comparisons. Only when we have closely and systematically examined over time the legislatures of most countries will we be able to stress precisely what their strong points are and to assess whether they achieve, in some polities at least, very marked results. But the idealized version of their role has probably been the greatest drawback to a realistic assessment. Because of a very short-sighted view of the means of achieving liberalism, it has been consistently held, almost as an axiom, that legislatures were both the necessary and sufficient condition to achieve liberalism. Parties are studied realistically, and it is normally agreed that they may be more or less open, more or less democratic, more or less responsive. Courts and even the press are ranked realistically, as if it was recognized that human failings lead to variations and that it is possible for some criticisms to be valid and thus for varying amounts of value to be attached to the institution. But with legislatures it has often seemed to be the case that they *had* to make constitutions and to make laws of their own free will, for only then could they achieve a real significance. The notion of "sovereignty" was assumed to imply either full power or total masquerade.

The quicker it becomes recognized by all, students and practitioners of politics alike, that legislatures are not sovereign because sovereignty is a meaningless concept in regard to any real system, the quicker the role of legislatures will become more apparent. The sooner it is recognized—not as fact that one must pessimistically "accept," but as an inescapable fact of life common to all human institutions—that there is nothing wrong in legislatures being under pressure, in rules being passed by a variety of bodies, only one of which is the legislature, the quicker it will become possible to come to a theory of legislative involvement which takes into account what legislatures are able to achieve and, indeed, do achieve in at least some countries.

Legislatures do not make laws in the full sense of the word. They cannot, incidentally, make constitutions either, though they are possibly slightly better equipped to do the latter than the former, because constitutions are legal documents which are changed only from time to time and, unlike most of the laws, do not require an administrative base which legislatures do not and cannot have. To state that legislatures are to make laws is to refuse to recognize that most legislation (except for legislation relating to private matters) implies a preparation at the technical level and a modicum of agreement between various interested parties which cannot be achieved in a legislature. Indeed, to prohibit civil servants from taking part in the preparation and drafting of the bills on the grounds that such activities infringe on the legislature's prerogatives would be a misuse of the resources available to the bureaucracy. It is therefore perfectly normal that the main rules of the country (whether or not they take the form of statutes) should be, on the whole, prepared, studied, and presented by the executive and not prepared in the legislature. It would be wholly abnormal for the legislature to make it a common practice to reject these laws or to amend them beyond recognition.

It is no more reasonable to expect legislatures to be involved in making and unmaking governments in a detailed and recurrent fashion. It is true that there should be a relationship between the legislature and the executive. This relationship is closer when the system is not of a presidential kind, though, even in these systems, many members of the executive proceed, directly or indirectly, from the legislature. But the dependence of the executive on the legislature cannot be expected to be very strong, for if it were, the consequence would be a series of upheavals which would not make for regularity in the leadership's conduct of the polity's public affairs. What is more, such an approach necessarily would affect policy-making inasmuch as more emphasis would be put on the problem of government making than on the content of governmental activities—which is necessarily slimmer when much of the executive's energies are bent on survival. Thus legislatures cannot be expected to do more than provide some guidance and a loose examination of the executive and its activities. Any other approach to the role of legislatures defeats the very purpose of representative government, for the executive would no longer "represent," but would dissolve itself into a series of Venetian activities where personality problems play a greater part than the defense or promotion of the people's interests.

The yardstick by which to measure the significance of legislatures should not be whether the legislature "really" passes all the statutes, or even most of the rules of the country, and whether it is in a "real" position to make and unmake governments. These simply are not the "functions" of legislatures. The function of the legislature is to provide a means of ensuring that there are channels of communication between the people and the executive, as a result of which it is possible for demands to be injected into the decision-making machinery whenever they exist and for the executive decisions to be checked if they raise difficulties, problems, and injustices. This is why it is critical that the legislature be involved in matters of detail and of relatively limited importance as much as with matters of general importance. This is why it is also critical that the legislature be concerned with decisions already made as well as with matters still under consideration. Indeed, this is, historically, why legislatures began, for the defense and protection of citizens against undue encroachments by the executive on detailed and limited questions was often much more visible to the average man than the preparation of bills and the development of general principles.

This is not to deny the importance to legislatures of their having the legal powers to pass laws nor to play down the usefulness of a parliamentary system which allows for governments to be overthrown by members of the assembly. Such residual powers are one of the means which make it easier for the legislature to have effective influence on the activities of the executives. They give occasions for participation; they make some tradeoffs possible between fields in which legislatures do not have legal rights to intervene and those in which they do. Indeed, this distinction between law and reality is quite important from a behavioral standpoint, and observers of legislative reality must see the give-and-take that results from it as one of the factors that keeps assemblies alive. This situation is difficult to understand for those who do not recognize the realities of human organizations, and it is also difficult to understand for those who are too deeply immersed in this reality. Assemblies cannot achieve their communicating functions unless they have legal powers of decision, any more than they can do so if they try to insist on exercising these decision powers often.

Viewed in this fashion, contemporary legislatures no longer appear to be of no importance and to have little significance. Through individuals and as a collective body, they perform functions of supervision of activities of the executive at various levels and inject into the system demands which are sufficiently supported by the population. It is sometimes suggested, in relation to the United Kingdom in particular, that legislators conduct a "permanent election campaign." This is in fact only one of the ways in which they act, and possibly not one of the most important ones, unless one gives to the word "election" a much broader meaning than the simple fact of allowing one group of politicians to displace another group. Perhaps it would be more accurate to say that they conduct a permanent "scrutinizing campaign" which, in relation to broadest policy issues, may be the same thing as conducting a "permanent election campaign," though all the broad policy issues do not lead to "elections," in large part because elections are fought on only a few problems even in those countries where problems play a part; and, in many polities elections do not in fact enable electors to deal with issues and merely regularize the selection of candidates by other bodies or have a personal aspect.

VARIATIONS IN THE SIGNIFICANCE AND EFFECTIVE ROLE OF LEGISLATURES

To state that legislatures have a function to fulfill is not to suggest that this function is equally well fulfilled in all the countries of the world which have legislatures. Variations in patterns of activities are vast. Some assemblies meet very infrequently; some concentrate on the discussion of laws at the expense of other activities, at least on a formal basis; and the number of bills passed by some assemblies is very much smaller than the number passed by others. What is more, the importance of these bills varies markedly and the extent of discussion of each bill is in some places much smaller than in others. But this was to be expected in view of the prevailing pessimism about legislatures. What was perhaps less expected was the fact that, on balance, the number of legislatures where the discussion of bills is adequate, where the number of discussions other than on legislation is significant, and where the total number of days of meeting is relatively large is far from being confined to the Western liberal democracies. Latin American countries and many Commonwealth countries of the Third World score fairly high to high on these indicators of activities, while French-speaking African countries and even some of the Communist countries show a tendency to be involved in the matters which come to them and affect the way in which aspects of policy are handled in the whole polity.

Many more studies, both single-country and cross-national, are needed before we become reasonably confident about the extent of activity and the levels of influence which correspond to these activities. Strictly, we should be able in the future to assign "points" to the various legislatures and to place them on a continuum of influence. Until this is done, we have to be content with broad typologies. In this context, it might be admissible to describe the legislatures of the contempoarary world under four broad headings.

1. The first and lowest type of legislature is that whose ostensible activities are very small and almost nonexistent and whose effectiveness and influence remain largely at the level of detailed matters and, to a relatively limited extent, at the level of intermediate questions. The most extreme example of such a legislature in the sample which we analyzed is that of East Germany. Undoubtedly, the Soviet Union's Supreme Soviet was in this group during the Stalin period, but there appears to be evidence showing some change in the course of the late 1950s and the 1960s, even though debates remain essentially formal except with respect to local and detailed issues. It seems that such legislatures may have a greater impact through their committees, whose activities are usually ill known and whose quantity of outputs is therefore impossible to measure adequately. All that is certain is that some changes take place as a result of the activities of committees at the intermediate level, but it is not yet clear how much total change is obtained and how much is rejected or not even put forward by the legislators. Clearly, such nascent or inchoate legislatures are not wholly rubber stamps, for they do perform a minimum of real functions; but they are nearer to "limited surgeries" or to "low-grade ombudsmen" than they are to legislatures in the proper sense of the word.

2. The second type is that of the legislature where a number of bills, and occasionally general policies, are discussed, and discussed with reasonable effectiveness, but where these constitute only a segment of the matters which "should" come to the legislature. These truncated legislatures have a degree of influence within the context of their activities, but it is difficult to grant them more than a limited influence overall inasmuch as they do not appear to concern themselves with some of the most important aspects of the life of the country, whether on foreign affairs or on broad social and economic matters. This situation seems to prevail in many African countries (possibly more in French-speaking countries than in Common-

wealth polities) as well as in some other countries such as Singapore where the legislature meets infrequently. This situation probably also obtains in the more traditional countries, though the absence of data on Jordan, Ethiopia, or Portugal makes it of course impossible to do more than suggest that they might come under this classification.[1]

The level of activity and influence of these legislatures is uniformly greater than that of the first group. Not only is the amount of real debate on intermediate matters which takes place on the floor of these Houses larger, but detailed matters seem also to be treated more systematically and more regularly. Questions tend to occur and members of assemblies are expected to discuss matters of local and individual interest with ministers and civil servants; indeed, references, to these discussions are made in the legislature. What appears lacking is the real discussion or debate on matters of general concern. The most that happens is a presentation of ideas by members of the government, but no discussion, or very little, takes place on the general matters and the area of legislative activity remains essentially at a low level.

3. The third type is that of the legislature which does discuss all matters of government and is therefore appreciably involved in general questions as well as intermediate matters but is not, for a variety of reasons, really equipped to influence the executive to any considerable extent on broader questions, even though it may be quite influential in intermediate matters—possibly because the executive realizes the political expediency of giving the legislature an appreciable say in this area. Latin American countries such as Uruguay and Venezuela, but probably not Chile, come in this category; some Commonwealth countries, such as India, also appear to be in this group, as do countries scattered across the world (e.g., Lebanon) where the life of the legislature has been relatively unimpaired.[2] Among Atlantic countries, France appears to be in this category since the beginning of the Fifth Republic, though there may be a tendency for a move to the fourth category since De Gaulle's retirement and death. It is sometimes difficult to make valid comparisons, because problems affecting smaller countries (e.g. Switzerland) are necessarily of relatively smaller importance than those affecting larger countries and a legislature such as the Swiss legislature may therefore appear unduly concerned with relatively unimportant or intermediate matters by comparison with the legislatures of larger countries. But on the whole, as a comparative study of the importance of bills in five countries showed, the problems raised in France were of some-

---

[1] The Portuguese National Assembly has shown some signs of greater liveliness since the disappearance of Salazar, especially in 1971.

[2] For a balanced conclusion on the Indian situation, see W. H. Morris-Jones, *Parliament in India* (London: Longmans, Green, and Co., Ltd., 1957).

what more limited importance than those raised in other European countries.[3] The amount of debate on matters other than legislation was relatively limited and more effort was made to discuss intermediate or even detailed questions than to discuss general matters.

The result is that these legislatures have fairly considerable influence in intermediate matters but very little influence, even in the long run, on general matters. They have some effective power in constraining executive legislation, but even this has its limits; they have very little power to initiate new ideas, and their initiative remains concentrated on intermediate questions. At the other end of the spectrum, however, such legislatures do seem to fulfill very adequately their functions in relation to detailed demands and the supervision of detailed outputs. The machinery for this job is there, and so is an expectation on the part of constituents that legislators will fulfill these functions. Questions are numerous, sometimes even very numerous; the access of legislators to ministerial departments is granted naturally and official arrangements are made for the channeling of complaints through legislators. These legislatures are more *inhibited* than truncated, in that they tread only warily into the field of general problems.

4. Lastly, most Western European legislatures, those of the older Commonwealth countries, and that of the United States can be said to fulfill in a generally adequate way the functions of channeling demands and discussing general problems as well as having various means of intervention in order to veto some of the more exaggerated suggestions of executive or in order to initiate a number of new ideas, even in the field of general matters. As we stated, it is very difficult to make definite assertions in this field; a much more comprehensive examination of activities over time is required before the exact amount of general influence, both negative and positive, is known. The United States Congress appears much "stronger" than many legislatures, but its influence is mostly negative and part of its strength stems from the fact that open disagreements with the executive are well documented, that most of the analysis is conducted on a yearly basis, and that the executive tries out ideas on Congress at a much earlier stage than European and Commonwealth executives do on their legislatures. The development of new ideas is slow in Congress, as it is in European legislatures; indeed, the influence of the President and the executive in general is often crucial if ideas are to succeed.

Because the model of lawmaking by legislatures is so deeply rooted in the minds of legislators and students of legislatures alike, it usually is stated that these legislatures achieve relatively little, that they lead to the frustration of members, and that they end up either in negative postures (as in the United States, pre-1958 France, and possiby Chile) or in servile acceptance

---

[3] See Chapter 6.

of executive suggestions. But, given the pressures on executive and legislature alike arising from "recurrent" problems, and given, on the other hand,
the influence which legislatures have in many detailed, intermediate, and
even new general matters, it does seem that these legislatures in fact come
fairly close to achieving their *true* functions. To be sure, improvements
could bring them closer, but these improvements would involve changes in
degree rather than changes in kind.

THE FUTURE OF LEGISLATURES

There is unquestionably a revived interest in legislatures among political scientists and observers of
politics. In the late 1960s there were moves in a
number of countries—among Western industrial democracies, in the Third World, and even in Eastern
Communist countries—to increase the role of legislatures. A number of
countries, as we noted in the first chapter, have reopened their legislatures
and the apparent drop in the overall percentage of countries with legislatures
seems to be caused primarily by a not unexpected drop in the number of
African legislatures. Even this drop now seems to be checked, with a revival
or creation of legislatures in countries as different and distant as Indonesia,
Upper Volta, Argentina, and even South Yemen. This is not to say that we
soon should expect all countries to have legislatures, let alone "functioning"
legislatures, that would be equally concerned with detailed, intermediate,
and general matters and would exercise their influence adequately at all
levels. It is to say that the long-term trend is not toward the disappearance
or even the "decline" of legislatures.

Moreover, as we have had occasion to notice, it usually is not sufficiently recognized that an institution such as a legislature has to grow
gradually, not only because it has to be accepted by executives, of which
many are authoritarian or "charismatic," but also because the legislators
themselves have to learn to act. Indeed, those entering the legislature have
to be turned gradually into legislators by the sheer development of the
institution itself. In the field of legislatures as in other fields of politics,
the tendency is too much to forget the difference between the short and the
long term as well as to forget the importance of the legitimization process
in its various forms, one of which could be described as the internal legitimization of an activity by the actors concerned. We noted the effects of this
long-term tendency on the career of legislators. It is not exaggerated to say
that when a legislature is created, and *a fortiori* when a country and a
legislature are created at the same time, there is no legislative career because
the actors themselves have not yet learned to think of the job as a career,
regardless of the electoral prospects and the institutional arrangements. The
establishment of a legislative is only slowly acquired, as the experience of

the countries which have had legislatures for a long time does more than just indicate.

It follows that, as the history of the legislature unfolds, its members will come gradually, by an automatic development, to acquire a taste for the job and to understand the meaning and purpose of being a legislator. This development is not helped particularly by the myths attached to the institution. The more it is suggested that the function of a legislator is to decide "freely" and in a "sovereign" fashion about all matters of state, the more legislators and potential legislators will find it difficult to adjust to the reality of their limited control over individual, intermediate, and general matters. But, the longer a legislature lasts, the more its members will adjust naturally to this reality, simply because the selection process will weed out those whose ambitions cannot be met and will replace them by men and women who have a more realistic vision of the role of assemblies.

This is perhaps particularly true in relation to broad policies, since, as we saw, legislatures of the "inhibited" type tend particularly to be inhibited because of the inability of the legislators themselves to consider the process of exerting pressure at the general level as one which takes place over a decade or more. This means that no change or influence at this level will take place if the legislators are not devoting their careers—or large parts of their careers—to the promotion of general ideas. They must not be in a hurry, which they will clearly be where the turnover of members is high. What is more, they must be prepared to concentrate their activities on a small number of ideas, or indeed perhaps one idea only, during most of the time during which they promote this idea. Therefore, they must have, consciously or unconsciously, a very strong feeling that most of the problems are of a "recurrent" type, that change at this level will be limited and highly technical, and that the executive necessarily will have a large share in these fields. Because such a socialization process requires time, it is not surprising that many legislatures have not yet adjusted, but there are good reasons to believe that adjustment will take place. Thus, unless the situation in the Fifth Republic in France reverts to a mode of behavior similar to the Fourth, it should be possible for French legislators, in the late 1970s and 1980s, to become adjusted to their "pressure" role in the realm of new ideas and thus to begin making their influence felt in a significant way.

Moreover, in a wide group of legislatures a distinct development is taking place with regard to intermediate matters. By a natural process, the role of the "charismatic" leaders who came at the time of independence in many Third World countries is beginning to decrease. In Tunisia or Yugoslavia, in Ghana or the Ivory Coast, efforts are being made for a variety of reasons, and usually in different ways, to increase the role of the legislature. In some cases these efforts take the form of ill-advised attempts to change the legislative personnel in order to obtain more "dedicated" members anxious to work for the public good and to work nearer to the constituents. Regardlessless of their form, however, these efforts suggest that there is a concern among "the political class" for the development of activities in the legislature and that legislators are likely in the long run to increase their influence at both the detailed and the intermediate levels. The development of committees in other states, such as the Soviet Union, seems also to point in the same direction. It may not be possible as yet for the legislatures of these polities to become markedly involved in broader policies. But, given that we know that time is required for such an involvement to become permanent and to "settle" at a stable point, the development of lower-key activities clearly will have a generally beneficial effect on the long-term influence of many legislatures.

The future of legislatures is therefore far from bleak. The time has surely passed when it was possible for students of individual countries to dismiss legislatures with a passing reference. What is required is a serious study of the various activities, a concern for the problems raised by detailed pressure, and an examination of the content of activities, on the floor and in committees, in most of the countries. Legislatures are an important channel of communication and pressure. Invented by mankind in the course of history for purposes of debate and discussion, they were temporarily, for very special reasons, given exalted missions which they could not fulfill. They have, nonetheless, survived. They have expanded their activities markedly in most of the countries where they were first given these exalted powers, despite many cries about their impotence and inadequacy. They have expanded elsewhere, often by sheer imitation, and it is not surprising that, in the majority of cases, they should not have adjusted easily to the new conditions. But there, too, they have survived, and only in a minority of cases has the implantation been wholly unsuccessful—and even in those cases not permanently so. As legislatures begin slowly to return to their role of communication and pressure in most of the polities, they are also slowly but increasingly seen to have "adequate" functions and a profound relevance. They will play a key part in the development of political societies in the coming decades.

CONSTITUTIONAL CHARACTERISTICS OF LEGISLATURES

A

A. The countries without legislatures at January 1, 1971 were:

Atlantic area: Greece

Eastern Europe and North Asia: nil

Middle East and North Africa: Algeria, Bahrein, Iraq, Libya, Morocco (in the process of being created), Muscat and Oman, Qatar, Saudi Arabia, South Yemen, Syria, Yemen

South and East Asia: Burma, Pakistan (in the process of being created)

Africa south of the Sahara: Burundi, Central African Republic, Congo-Brazzaville, Congo-Kinshasa, Dahomey, Mali, Nigeria, Somalia, Sudan, Togo, Uganda, Upper Volta (in the process of being created)

Latin America: Argentia, Bolivia (a "popular" assembly was in being), Cuba, Peru

B. The constitutional characteristics which follow are given for the other 108 countries, on the basis of the following codes:

Col 1–3:	Country identification (alphabetical)
Col 4–7:	Population (in hundred thousands)
Col 8–10:	Size of lower chamber
Col 11–14:	Ratio of size of lower chamber to population (in hundred thousands)
Col 15:	Second chamber:
	1: No
	2: Yes
Col 16–18:	Size of second chamber
Col 19–22:	Ratio of combined size of the two chambers to population (in hundred thousands)
Col 23:	Voting restrictions:
	1: Full universal suffrage
	2: Literacy requirements
	3: Male only
	4: Racial restrictions
	5: Property and race restrictions

6:    Literacy, property, and race restrictions
7:    Property and race restrictions, also male only
9:    Not ascertainable
(These are the only restrictions which exist in fact in the contemporary world; codes for other possible restrictions therefore are not given.)

Col 24:   Party system
           1:    No parties
           2:    Full single-party system
           3:    Forced coalition of parties under the aegis of one dominant party
           4:    Dominant single-party system
           5:    Two-party system (balanced or unbalanced)
           6:    Two-and-a-half-party system
           7:    Multi-party system with a dominant party (other than 3)
           8:    Multi-party system without a dominant party

Col 25:   Monarchical or republican form of government:
           1:    Monarchy
           2:    Republic
           3:    Ambiguous (Spain)

Col 26:   Structure of state:
           1:    Unitary
           2:    Federal

Col 27:   Parliamentary immunity:
           1:    Full
           2:    Some accountability to the house
           3:    None
           9:    Not ascertainable

Col 28:   Parliamentary inviolability:
           1:    Full
           2:    With authorization of the house
           3:    None
           9:    Not ascertainable

Col 29:   Procedural independence:
           1:    Full
           2:    Shared
           3:    None
           9:    Not ascertainable

Col 30:   Type of session:
           1:    Permanent
           2:    Periods designated in the constitution
           3:    Session opened and closed at will by head of state
           9:    Not ascertainable

Col 31:   Emergency powers:
           1:    The executive may issue provisional laws at any time on any matter
           2:    The executive may issue provisional laws under some restrictions
           3:    The executive may not issue provisional laws
           9:    Not ascertainable

Col 32:   Referendums:
                  1: None
                  2: On constitutional matters only
                  3: Both on constitutional and on some legislative matters
                  4: Mentioned without details
                  9: Not ascertainable

Col 33–34:   Majority for constitutional change:
                  (If more than one step, the second column is used; if only
                  one, the second column is punched "0.")
                  10: Simple majority
                  20: Three-fifths
                  30: Two-thirds
                  40: Three-quarters
                  50: Special meetings of two houses
                  60: Approval of states or provinces
                  70: Setting up of constitutent assemblies
                  80: Referendum
                  99: Not ascertainable

Col 35:   Entrenched clauses:
                  1: None
                  2: For some minority groups or areas
                  3: For some clauses
                  9: Not ascertainable

Col 36:   Constitutional·court:
                  1: Yes, appointed by executive
                  2: Yes, appointed by executive and ratified by assembly
                  3: Yes, appointment shared by executive and assembly
                  4: Yes, appointed by assembly alone
                  5: Yes, appointment not specified
                  9: No court mentioned

Col 37:   Basis of selection of second chamber:
                  1: Hereditary or appointed by executive
                  2: Members chosen by constituencies in proportion to
                      population
                  3: Selection favoring rural areas, villages, etc.
                  4: Selection favoring or based on states, provinces, etc.
                  5: Selection giving equal number to states, provinces, etc.
                  6: Numbers 1 & 2
                  7: Numbers 1 & 4
                  8: Numbers 1 & 5
                  9: No second chamber

Col 38:   Powers of second chamber:
                  1: Stronger than first
                  2: Equal to first
                  3: Can be overriden
                  4: Only with advisory powers
                  9: No second chamber

Col 39:   Selection of head of state:
                  1: Popular suffrage
                  2: Electoral college

	3: Legislature
	4: Executive
	5: Self-appointed
	6: Hereditary
Col 40:	Ministers in legislature
	1: Have to be members of legislature
	2: May attend legislature, but appointed from without
	3: May attend and may be members of legislature
	4: Not members and may not attend legislature
	9: Not ascertainable
Col 41:	Dissolution:
	1: Specifically stated that no dissolution is allowed
	2: At discretion of legislature only
	3: At discretion of executive but in some circumstances only
	4: At full discretion of executive
	5: Automatic in some circumstances
	6: Numbers 2 & 5
	9: Not ascertainable
Col 42:	Censure and resignation of executive:
	1: No power stated or only inquiry
	2: Special procedure for censure, but executive must resign
	3: No special procedure
	4: Impeachment only
	5: Numbers 3 & 4
	6: Numbers 2 & 4
	9: Not ascertainable
Col 43:	Fields of legislation:
	1: Power of legislature to pass laws complete
	2: Restrictions on lawmaking powers of legislature in internal and external matters
	3: Restrictions on lawmaking powers of legislature on external matters only
	9: Not ascertainable
Col 44:	Right to request the legislature to reread a bill:
	1: Yes, granted to executive
	2: No
	9: Not ascertainable
Col 45:	Veto:
	1: Full veto
	2: Restrictions in some fields
	3: Can be overriden by legislature
	9: No veto mentioned

Atlantic Area

	1	2	3	4	5	6	7	8	9	10	11	12	13	14	15	16	17	18	19	20	21	22	23	24	25	26	27	28	29	30	31	32	33	34	35	36	37	38	39	40	41	42	43	44	45
Australia	0	0	5	0	1	1	6	1	2	4	0	1	0	5	2	0	6	0	0	4	8	5	1	1	2	1	9	2	2	7	8	3	1	5	3	1	6	1	4	3	2	1	9		
Austria	0	0	6	0	0	7	2	1	6	5	0	2	3	0	2	0	5	4	0	3	5	6	5	2	2	1	9	2	9	3	3	8	1	3	4	3	1	3	4	3	1	2	9		
Belgium	0	0	9	0	0	0	9	5	2	2	0	2	2	2	1	0	7	8	0	4	0	1	6	1	1	1	2	9	9	9	5	0	1	9	9	9	1	6	3	4	1	2	9		
Canada	0	1	9	0	2	0	3	2	6	5	0	3	3	5	0	1	8	2	4	8	5	0	6	1	2	1	1	2	9	9	1	8	0	1	3	6	3	6	4	4	1	1	3		
Denmark	0	3	4	0	0	4	7	1	7	9	0	8	8	0	2	1	9	9	2	0	8	1	7	6	1	1	3	1	2	3	1	8	0	9	9	3	6	3	4	5	3	2	9		
Eire	0	3	7	0	0	2	8	1	7	0	0	6	4	0	1	0	9	9	0	8	0	1	6	2	1	2	1	2	2	3	1	8	0	9	9	9	1	4	3	1	2	9			
Finland	0	4	1	0	0	4	6	2	0	0	0	4	3	5	2	0	6	9	0	4	3	1	8	1	1	2	1	2	2	3	1	8	0	3	3	9	1	3	4	5	1	2	3		
France	0	4	2	0	4	9	1	4	8	0	0	0	9	8	2	2	6	3	0	3	5	1	7	8	2	1	2	2	3	1	8	0	0	3	4	3	1	2	4	2	1	1	9		
Germany, West	0	4	6	0	5	7	6	5	0	0	0	8	0	7	2	0	4	1	0	0	9	6	7	6	2	2	1	2	3	1	8	1	3	4	3	2	3	3	4	1	1	3			
Iceland	0	5	5	0	5	0	2	0	4	0	0	2	0	1	0	2	3	0	0	0	0	1	7	2	1	2	2	3	3	0	8	3	0	3	9	3	3	4	1	1	1	9			
Italy	0	6	1	0	5	0	2	9	6	3	0	1	1	0	2	3	5	1	3	7	8	1	7	1	1	1	2	3	9	9	3	0	3	9	2	2	3	4	3	1	2	9			
Luxembourg	0	7	5	0	0	0	3	0	5	6	1	8	6	0	1	9	9	9	1	8	6	1	6	1	1	2	2	3	3	9	8	1	9	9	9	6	2	4	4	1	2	9			
Malta	0	8	5	0	0	0	3	0	5	0	6	6	6	0	9	9	9	9	0	6	6	1	5	1	2	9	3	9	4	3	8	1	2	9	2	2	9	4	4	1	9	1			
Netherlands	0	8	9	0	1	2	5	1	5	0	1	0	0	0	2	0	7	5	1	8	0	1	8	1	1	1	2	1	3	1	3	3	1	9	9	2	6	6	4	3	1	2	9		
New Zealand	0	9	0	0	0	2	7	0	8	0	0	0	2	5	1	9	2	9	0	9	5	1	7	1	1	1	2	1	3	9	9	9	0	1	9	9	6	6	4	4	1	1	3		
Norway	0	9	4	0	0	0	3	6	1	5	0	4	1	5	2	2	3	8	0	5	6	1	6	2	1	2	2	1	2	3	1	9	3	1	9	2	3	6	2	2	1	2	9		
Portugal	1	0	1	0	0	0	9	2	1	0	0	1	4	0	2	2	0	0	0	6	0	2	3	3	1	2	1	2	2	9	2	2	8	3	3	4	4	2	2	4	2	1	2	3	
Spain	1	1	3	0	3	1	6	6	0	0	0	0	0	9	2	1	9	9	0	0	0	3	1	2	1	2	1	2	2	1	3	9	8	1	5	9	9	5	5	4	3	2	1	1	
Sweden	1	6	0	0	7	8	3	5	0	0	0	4	5	0	1	9	9	9	0	4	0	1	7	2	2	2	2	2	2	2	3	9	9	1	9	9	9	9	3	9	4	2	9	9	
Switzerland	1	7	0	0	5	5	2	0	0	0	3	6	0	2	1	8	4	0	4	6	0	8	1	1	2	1	9	3	2	1	1	8	0	3	4	5	2	3	6	9	1	1	2	9	
UK	1	8	5	4	7	6	3	0	0	0	1	5	2	2	8	8	0	0	6	0	1	5	2	1	2	1	3	2	3	1	3	1	3	6	1	9	1	3	6	1	4	3	2	3	
US	1	2	9	1	9	5	3	4	3	5	0	2	2	2	1	1	0	0	8	2	8	1	5	2	2	2	1	2	9	2	9	4	1	6	1	5	2	2	5	1	9	4	2	1	3

East Europe and North Asia

	1	2	3	4	5	6	7	8	9	10	11	12	13	14	15	16	17	18	19	20	21	22	23	24	25	26	27	28	29	30	31	32	33	34	35	36	37	38	39	40	41	42	43	44	45
Albania	0	0	2	0	0	1	4	1	9	2	1	3	8	0	1	9	9	9	1	3	8	0	1	2	2	1	1	3	1	2	2	3	3	8	1	9	9	9	3	3	3	3	3	2	9
Bulgaria	0	1	4	0	0	8	2	4	1	6	0	5	1	0	1	9	9	9	0	5	0	0	1	2	2	1	1	2	1	2	2	4	3	0	1	9	9	9	3	3	3	3	2	2	9
China	0	2	5	6	9	0	0	8	8	8	0	1	1	0	1	9	1	5	0	0	3	0	1	1	2	1	9	9	9	1	1	9	2	0	0	1	5	2	3	9	9	9	1	9	9
Czechoslovakia	0	3	2	0	1	4	2	3	0	0	0	2	1	0	2	1	5	0	0	3	2	0	1	3	2	1	2	2	1	2	2	3	2	0	1	9	5	2	3	3	6	2	3	2	9
Germany, East	0	4	5	0	1	7	3	4	0	0	0	3	0	0	1	9	9	9	0	0	3	0	1	1	2	1	2	1	2	2	2	9	3	8	1	4	9	9	9	3	1	6	1	2	9
Hungary	0	5	4	0	1	0	1	3	4	0	0	3	5	0	1	9	9	9	0	3	5	0	1	1	2	1	1	2	1	2	2	9	3	0	1	9	9	9	3	3	3	3	3	2	9
North Korea	0	6	7	0	1	1	8	3	3	0	0	2	0	0	1	9	9	9	0	3	2	0	1	1	2	1	1	2	1	2	9	9	3	0	1	9	9	9	3	3	1	3	2	2	9
Mongolia	0	8	5	0	0	3	1	2	8	7	0	6	0	0	1	9	9	9	2	6	3	0	1	1	2	1	1	9	0	2	9	9	3	0	1	9	9	9	3	3	1	9	3	2	9
Poland	1	0	0	0	3	5	0	4	6	0	0	1	3	0	1	9	9	9	0	0	6	0	1	2	2	1	9	2	1	2	9	9	3	0	1	9	9	9	3	3	1	3	3	2	9
Rumania	1	0	4	0	1	9	1	4	4	6	0	2	4	5	1	9	9	7	2	4	5	1	1	2	2	1	1	2	1	2	1	4	3	0	1	9	9	9	3	1	3	3	3	2	9
USSR	1	2	6	2	3	4	4	7	5	5	0	3	2	2	2	2	6	7	0	0	2	5	1	2	2	2	9	2	2	2	4	4	3	4	1	9	4	2	3	3	5	5	9	2	9
North Vietnam	1	3	3	0	1	7	0	3	6	6	0	2	1	5	1	1	9	6	0	1	9	0	1	2	2	2	2	9	9	2	9	9	9	0	1	9	9	9	3	9	9	3	9	9	9
Yugoslavia	1	3	7	0	1	9	2	1	2	0	0	0	6	2	2	6	0	0	0	3	1	0	2	2	2	2	1	1	1	2	2	2	2	8	1	4	2	2	3	3	3	3	1	2	9

Middle East and North Africa

	1	2	3	4	5	6	7	8	9	10	11	12	13	14	15	16	17	18	19	20	21	22	23	24	25	26	27	28	29	30	31	32	33	34	35	36	37	38	39	40	41	42	43	44	45
Afghanistan	0	0	1	0	1	5	2	2	1	7	0	1	4	0	2	0	4	5	0	1	7	6	1	1	1	1	1	2	1	2	2	7	3	3	3	9	7	3	6	3	4	5	1	1	3
Cyprus	0	3	1	0	0	6	0	5	0	0	0	8	4	0	1	9	9	9	8	4	4	1	1	4	2	1	1	1	1	2	1	3	0	3	2	1	9	9	2	2	2	2	2	3	2
Iran	0	5	8	0	0	2	5	7	2	0	0	7	8	0	2	0	6	0	0	8	0	0	1	1	1	9	9	2	1	2	9	9	9	9	3	9	6	2	6	2	4	5	2	1	9
Israel	0	6	0	0	0	0	5	1	2	2	4	0	0	0	1	0	9	0	4	0	8	0	1	7	2	1	1	1	2	2	9	9	7	9	9	6	2	6	3	3	2	3	1	2	9
Jordan	0	6	5	0	0	2	0	0	6	0	3	0	0	0	1	9	9	9	0	5	0	0	3	1	1	1	1	2	1	2	1	3	9	3	5	3	1	3	6	3	3	3	3	1	3
Kuwait	0	6	9	0	0	0	0	5	0	0	0	3	0	0	1	9	9	9	4	0	5	0	0	1	1	1	1	2	1	2	1	0	5	0	1	5	9	9	9	3	4	3	2	1	3
Lebanon	0	7	1	0	0	2	3	0	9	9	0	3	0	0	1	9	9	9	0	5	0	0	1	8	1	1	1	2	1	2	9	9	3	9	1	9	9	9	2	4	4	6	3	1	9
Tunisia	1	2	3	0	0	4	7	0	9	9	0	2	4	2	1	9	5	0	2	1	0	0	1	0	2	1	1	1	1	2	9	9	9	3	1	9	9	2	3	3	2	9	1	9	3
Turkey	1	2	4	0	3	1	4	4	5	0	0	1	1	8	1	9	9	9	1	1	1	0	5	1	1	1	1	1	1	2	9	3	0	0	3	3	7	3	3	3	3	6	1	6	9
U.A.R.	1	2	7	0	2	9	6	3	5	0	1	1	8	0	1	9	9	0	1	1	8	1	1	2	1	1	1	2	1	2	4	3	8	1	1	9	9	1	3	4	4	5	1	1	3

South and East Asia

	1	2	3	4	5	6	7	8	9	10	11	12	13	14	15	16	17	18	19	20	21	22	23	24	25	26	27	28	29	30	31	32	33	34	35	36	37	38	39	40	41	42	43	44	45
Bhutan	0	1	0	0	0	0	0	7	1	4	0	2	0	0	1	9	9	2	0	0	0	0	9	1	1	1	1	2	2	9	9	2	3	8	9	9	9	9	6	3	4	2	9	2	9
Cambodia	0	1	7	0	0	6	3	0	8	2	0	1	3	0	2	9	2	4	1	6	8	8	1	1	2	1	1	2	1	9	1	3	3	0	1	9	9	3	3	3	3	3	9	9	9
Ceylon	0	2	1	0	1	0	6	1	0	5	0	0	0	0	2	0	9	0	0	3	5	5	1	6	2	1	1	2	9	9	9	1	3	3	0	6	7	6	3	3	4	3	3	1	3
China (Taiwan)	0	2	4	0	1	3	0	4	5	7	0	0	5	0	2	9	2	9	0	5	0	5	0	1	2	2	1	9	1	2	2	3	4	0	3	1	6	6	6	3	4	1	1	1	1
India	0	5	6	4	9	9	8	5	2	5	0	3	1	0	1	2	9	0	0	0	2	0	9	7	2	1	1	2	9	2	2	9	3	8	1	7	3	3	2	1	4	5	9	1	9
Indonesia	0	5	7	0	6	0	2	3	9	0	0	0	2	2	1	2	5	0	0	0	7	2	9	2	4	2	1	9	1	2	9	2	3	0	1	9	1	2	9	9	9	1	9	9	9
Japan	0	6	4	0	9	8	7	4	6	7	0	0	4	6	2	9	9	0	0	0	0	0	1	5	1	1	1	1	1	2	2	1	3	3	3	2	1	3	3	3	9	3	1	1	1
South Korea	0	6	8	0	2	9	2	1	7	5	0	0	6	0	2	9	9	2	0	0	6	0	6	1	2	1	1	9	2	9	2	9	3	8	0	1	2	3	6	3	3	6	9	1	3
Laos	0	7	0	0	0	2	5	0	5	9	0	2	3	0	2	0	9	2	0	2	8	5	1	5	1	1	1	1	1	2	1	2	5	0	3	9	8	2	2	4	6	3	9	3	3
Malaysia	0	7	8	0	0	0	0	1	5	9	0	1	6	5	2	9	2	9	2	0	0	0	6	1	1	1	1	2	1	2	9	5	3	3	3	9	9	3	1	3	3	9	9	9	9
Maldive Islands	0	7	9	0	0	0	2	0	5	4	2	7	0	5	1	1	9	7	0	2	8	0	1	6	2	2	1	9	1	9	9	1	3	9	0	2	9	3	1	4	2	2	3	1	1
Nepal	0	8	0	0	9	4	1	2	5	0	0	0	3	4	2	9	9	9	1	0	3	4	1	1	1	2	9	2	9	3	1	9	9	0	1	9	9	9	9	2	9	2	2	2	3
Philippines	0	9	0	0	3	4	6	4	6	0	0	2	2	2	2	0	2	4	0	1	8	8	9	2	2	1	9	1	2	2	2	2	5	8	1	2	3	3	1	2	1	4	1	1	3
Singapore	1	0	9	0	0	1	9	0	5	1	0	7	7	0	1	9	8	0	0	2	7	0	1	4	1	1	9	1	1	9	9	9	1	0	9	9	1	9	6	1	9	2	1	1	9
Thailand	1	2	0	0	1	8	2	4	0	0	0	0	5	2	0	6	0	0	1	4	4	8	2	2	1	2	1	2	1	2	2	2	3	8	0	4	3	3	2	2	4	3	3	1	3
South Vietnam	1	3	4	0	1	6	1	2	3	7	0	8	5	0	1	9	6	0	0	1	9	9	9	1	1	1	1	2	1	2	3	3	2	3	3	4	1	6	2	1	2	6	3	1	3
West Samoa	1	3	5	0	0	0	1	0	4	7	4	0	0	0	1	0	9	4	7	0	0	0	7	1	1	1	9	1	1	2	2	2	3	8	1	1	9	9	3	3	4	1	2	3	1

Africa South of the Sahara

	1	2	3	4	5	6	7	8	9	10	11	12	13	14	15	16	17	18	19	20	21	22	23	24	25	26	27	28	29	30	31	32	33	34	35	36	37	38	39	40	41	42	43	44	45
Botswana	0	1	2	0	0	0	6	0	3	6	0	6	0	0	2	0	1	5	0	8	4	0	1	5	2	1	9	9	9	9	9	9	9	9	9	9	3	3	3	3	4	3	3	1	3
Cameroon	0	1	8	0	0	5	5	0	5	5	0	0	2	0	0	9	9	9	0	0	0	0	1	5	2	1	1	9	1	2	2	4	1	0	3	9	9	9	1	2	9	1	2	1	9
Chad	0	2	2	0	0	0	2	0	5	0	0	2	7	1	1	9	9	9	0	0	0	9	0	4	2	1	1	9	9	2	2	9	4	8	9	9	9	9	2	9	9	6	2	9	9
Equatorial Guinea	0	4	0	0	0	0	0	3	1	0	1	0	6	1	9	0	0	6	2	1	5	0	1	1	1	1	2	1	1	1	2	9	9	9	3	9	5	1	6	2	3	4	2	9	3
Ethiopia	0	3	9	0	2	2	5	2	0	7	0	9	9	4	2	0	5	5	0	1	4	7	9	1	4	1	9	9	9	9	9	9	4	5	9	9	9	2	9	4	4	4	9	9	3
Gabon	0	4	3	0	0	0	4	0	4	1	0	0	1	0	1	9	9	9	0	8	8	0	9	5	1	1	1	9	1	2	2	2	3	3	3	5	1	1	1	3	4	4	2	1	3
Gambia	0	4	4	0	0	0	3	0	4	3	0	3	4	2	9	0	9	9	0	0	0	0	0	2	2	1	1	9	1	2	2	2	3	0	3	9	9	6	2	1	4	4	9	1	9
Ghana	0	4	7	0	0	0	7	9	7	4	0	1	7	8	1	0	9	9	0	2	1	8	0	0	2	1	1	2	1	2	2	2	3	8	3	9	9	9	2	3	9	5	2	9	1
Guinea	0	5	0	0	0	3	5	0	7	0	0	2	1	5	1	9	9	9	2	0	7	5	1	2	2	1	1	2	9	2	2	2	3	8	9	9	9	9	2	2	9	2	2	9	9
Ivory Coast	0	6	2	0	0	4	1	0	1	5	0	0	0	1	1	0	9	9	0	2	0	2	0	4	2	1	1	9	9	2	2	9	2	9	3	5	9	1	9	9	9	4	9	9	3
Kenya	0	6	6	0	0	0	1	1	8	5	0	1	8	6	1	9	9	9	2	0	0	6	0	4	4	1	1	1	9	2	2	2	3	3	3	9	9	1	9	2	9	4	9	1	3
Lesotho	0	7	2	0	0	0	9	9	0	0	0	6	7	1	1	2	3	3	1	1	8	6	5	4	2	1	1	9	9	2	2	9	9	9	9	9	9	9	6	1	4	3	4	9	3
Liberia	0	7	3	0	0	1	0	0	4	1	0	4	0	0	0	0	8	8	0	5	9	0	0	5	2	1	1	1	1	2	2	9	9	3	1	3	5	2	1	5	9	4	2	1	9
Madagascar	0	7	6	0	0	6	5	0	5	0	0	1	6	1	2	0	4	4	1	2	4	4	5	2	2	1	1	2	9	2	2	9	3	0	3	8	9	1	1	2	3	6	2	1	9
Malawi	0	7	7	0	0	0	4	0	0	5	0	1	3	8	9	0	9	9	0	1	3	8	2	2	2	1	1	2	9	2	2	2	3	8	9	5	9	3	1	1	4	4	4	1	1
Mauritania	0	8	2	0	0	0	9	0	4	0	0	4	4	0	0	0	9	9	0	4	7	0	0	5	2	1	1	1	1	2	2	1	9	9	9	9	9	1	9	1	9	4	2	1	9
Mauritius	0	8	3	0	0	0	8	0	7	0	0	8	7	2	1	0	9	9	0	8	8	0	9	2	2	1	1	2	1	2	9	9	4	8	9	9	9	9	6	2	9	9	9	9	3
Niger	0	9	2	0	0	4	0	0	7	0	0	0	4	4	4	0	9	9	0	0	4	4	1	5	5	1	1	1	9	2	9	3	3	9	9	9	9	9	2	1	9	9	2	9	9
Rhodesia	1	0	3	0	0	4	3	0	6	6	0	1	7	1	1	3	9	9	0	1	5	3	3	4	4	1	1	9	9	2	9	4	4	8	9	3	3	3	1	2	4	9	2	9	9
Rwanda	1	0	5	0	0	0	0	0	0	4	0	5	5	6	1	0	9	9	0	1	5	6	6	5	2	1	1	9	1	2	2	2	3	0	3	5	9	1	1	1	5	6	2	1	3
Senegal	1	0	7	0	0	3	5	0	7	7	0	1	5	6	1	0	9	9	0	1	4	1	0	5	2	1	1	9	1	2	9	3	3	3	3	5	3	9	9	2	9	4	2	1	1
Sierra Leone	1	0	8	0	0	2	2	0	6	6	0	0	3	0	0	0	5	5	0	3	2	0	4	5	2	1	1	9	9	2	9	2	1	0	1	3	5	6	6	1	4	3	2	3	9
South Africa	1	1	1	0	1	6	0	1	7	0	0	1	0	6	8	0	4	4	0	0	0	0	0	4	5	1	1	1	9	2	9	1	9	9	0	5	7	3	1	1	3	1	3	1	3
Swaziland	1	1	5	0	0	0	4	0	3	7	0	7	5	0	2	0	4	4	1	1	0	5	1	4	2	1	1	9	9	9	9	9	9	0	9	9	1	6	3	1	9	1	9	9	9
Tanzania	1	1	9	0	1	3	9	1	0	0	0	1	0	7	0	1	9	9	0	0	7	0	0	4	2	1	1	9	1	2	9	9	9	9	1	9	3	3	1	4	4	4	9	9	3
Zambia	1	3	8	0	0	3	9	0	5	0	0	2	7	0	1	9	9	0	2	7	0	1	4	2	1	1	9	9	3	2	2	3	3	8	1	9	9	1	9	4	1	1	1	3

Latin America

	1	2	3	4	5	6	7	8	9	10	11	12	13	14	15	16	17	18	19	20	21	22	23	24	25	26	27	28	29	30	31	32	33	34	35	36	37	38	39	40	41	42	43	44	45
Barbados	0	0	8	0	0	0	0	2	0	4	1	2	0	0	2	0	0	2	2	2	2	0	1	6	5	1	9	1	9	2	3	1	9	0	0	3	1	3	6	4	4	1	3	1	1
Brazil	0	1	3	0	8	7	0	4	9	2	0	0	4	7	2	0	6	6	0	0	5	4	5	5	2	2	2	2	1	9	3	9	5	8	3	9	5	2	2	2	9	4	1	1	3
Chile	0	2	3	0	0	8	5	1	4	7	0	0	7	2	2	1	9	5	0	2	2	2	2	7	2	2	1	2	1	2	3	2	5	0	3	2	2	2	1	2	4	4	2	1	3
Colombia	0	2	6	0	1	7	8	1	9	0	0	1	0	2	2	0	0	5	0	1	6	6	6	5	2	1	1	1	1	2	1	3	0	8	0	4	0	2	2	2	4	4	2	1	3
Costa Rica	0	2	9	0	0	1	1	4	0	5	0	0	5	5	1	1	9	9	0	4	0	5	1	5	2	1	1	2	1	2	1	1	3	3	3	1	9	9	1	2	4	4	3	1	3
Dominican Rep.	0	3	5	0	0	3	6	0	7	4	0	4	0	0	2	0	0	2	0	2	8	4	4	5	8	1	1	1	2	2	2	3	0	3	1	5	5	3	1	2	9	5	2	1	3
Ecuador	0	3	6	0	0	5	0	0	7	2	0	2	4	4	2	0	0	7	0	2	0	0	7	2	6	1	1	1	1	2	1	0	3	5	0	9	5	2	2	2	1	5	2	1	3
El Salvador	0	3	8	0	0	3	0	0	5	2	0	0	1	7	2	1	5	5	0	0	2	2	4	6	2	2	1	2	1	2	9	1	5	8	3	3	4	2	2	2	9	1	2	1	3
Guatemala	0	4	9	0	0	4	4	0	0	5	0	0	2	2	1	1	9	9	0	1	4	0	0	2	2	1	1	1	1	2	1	1	1	0	3	4	9	9	3	1	3	6	1	1	3
Guyana	0	5	1	0	0	0	6	0	0	5	0	0	8	0	1	9	9	9	0	8	0	6	2	6	2	1	1	1	1	2	1	9	7	8	0	4	9	9	1	1	4	3	2	1	2
Haiti	0	5	3	0	0	0	0	5	8	3	0	8	2	6	1	0	9	9	0	2	6	0	6	2	2	1	1	1	2	2	9	1	1	0	3	0	9	9	1	1	2	4	1	1	2
Honduras	0	5	3	0	0	2	3	0	6	4	0	0	2	8	1	0	9	9	0	4	1	1	4	4	2	1	1	1	1	2	1	3	3	0	3	1	1	1	6	2	2	3	1	1	2
Jamaica	0	6	3	0	0	1	8	0	0	3	0	0	8	0	2	9	9	1	0	0	6	0	0	5	1	2	2	2	9	9	2	2	6	8	1	9	3	6	1	2	1	1	1	1	2
Mexico	0	8	4	0	0	1	1	0	2	1	0	0	5	5	2	0	2	0	0	3	3	6	2	4	2	2	1	1	1	2	2	9	5	0	1	2	5	2	2	2	5	5	4	1	2
Nicaragua	0	9	1	0	0	4	1	0	0	2	0	0	2	1	2	0	0	6	0	4	4	0	4	4	4	2	1	1	1	2	2	1	9	7	1	2	2	1	2	2	9	4	2	1	2
Panama	0	9	6	0	0	1	2	0	5	3	0	0	4	4	0	0	9	9	0	4	5	0	0	8	8	2	1	1	2	2	2	5	0	5	1	2	2	3	2	2	9	4	2	1	3
Paraguay	0	9	7	0	0	2	0	0	3	6	0	0	3	0	2	0	0	3	0	4	5	0	1	0	2	1	2	1	2	1	1	9	5	7	3	9	9	2	2	2	4	2	3	1	3
Trinidad & Tobago	1	2	2	0	0	0	0	3	0	3	0	0	4	2	1	2	0	4	0	7	0	0	5	1	6	2	2	1	1	2	1	0	3	3	3	2	3	3	6	1	4	2	1	9	3
Uruguay	1	3	1	0	0	2	7	0	9	9	0	3	6	3	2	0	2	4	0	5	8	0	1	5	1	1	1	1	9	2	1	2	8	8	8	9	2	2	1	1	2	3	6	1	3
Venezuela	1	3	2	0	0	8	7	1	3	3	0	5	3	2	0	0	5	1	0	2	1	2	1	7	2	2	1	2	1	2	2	1	5	6	1	4	5	2	1	2	9	6	3	1	3

ACTIVITIES
OF LEGISLATURES
LOWER HOUSES
B

Activities of Legislatures (Lower Houses)

		1 Date of observation	2 No. of days of sittings p.a.	3 No. of hours of sittings	4 Hours	5 Average daily sitting (hrs. mns.)	6 No. of bills passed each year (exc. finance)	7 No. of cttees.	8 Ratio of no. of cttees. to no. of members. %	9 Time for members per bill (mns.)	10 % of members who participate on floor	11 Average no. of daily divisions
Atlantic Area	Australia	1955–65	65	390	3.10	6.00	62	3	2	0.75		1.5
	Austria	1968–69					159	18	11			
	Canada	1966–68	180		2.30	6.00	75	17	6		95	
	Ireland	1965					34	0	0			
	France	1966	75	483	1.00	6.25	147	6	1	0.18	77	0.9
	Germany, West	1954	55	273	6.55							
	New Zealand	1964	90	550		6.05	119 (1965)	18	23			0.13(1965)
	Sweden	1966					285	10	4			
	Switzerland	1970	33	175	0.50	5.20	32	12	6	1.0	83	2.0
	UK	1962–69	160	1480	2.20	9.15	49	10–12	2	1.1	95(1954)	2.0
	US	1968	139	726	1.50	4.55	308	20	4			1.7
Eastern Europe	Germany, East	1970	3	10	0.01	3.20	4	10	3	0.18	8	0
	Hungary	1970	9	AB 40	0.07	4.25	3–4	19	4			0
	Poland	1961–65	10	AB 40	0.05	5.00						0?
	USSR	1966–70	13	90	0.07	7.00	6	12	2	0.04	15	0
	Yugoslavia	1969	18	75	0.40	4.10	15	12	10	0.6	40	?
Middle East and North Africa	Lebanon	1966	38				AB 100	8	9			
	Tunisia	1969–70	18	59	0.40	3.20	32					

Activities of Legislatures (Lower Houses) (continued)

Region		1 Date of observation	2 No. of days of sittings p.a.	3 No. of hours of sittings	4 Hours	5 Average daily sitting (hrs. mns.)	6 No. of bills passed each year (exc. finance)	7 No. of cttees.	8 Ratio of no. of cttees. to members %	9 Time for members per bill (mns.)	10 % of members who participate on floor	11 Average no. of daily divisions
South and Southeast Asia	India	1962–66	119	770	1.30	6.30	57	8	2	0.35	83(based on guests)	
	Philippines	1967	AB 100				231					
	Singapore	1969	9	30	0.35	3.20	24			1.1	69	0.25
	West Samoa	1969	35	122	2.35	3.30	24	5	10	2.1	90	0.45
Africa South of Sahara	Kenya	1969	74	283	1.40	3.50	17	1	1	3.0	50	0.8(1964)
	Madagascar	1968–69	11	36	0.20	3.20	27	9	8	0.5	64	0.3
	Senegal	1963	25	50	0.40	2.00	81	10	12	0.3		0.1
	Tanzania	1968	39									
	Zambia	1970	44	181	1.45	4.05	34			1.5	83	
Latin America	Chile	1963	54	260	1.45	4.50	50?			AB 1.00		4
	Colombia	1960s	136	AB 230								
	Costa Rica	1969		AB 500		.205		7	4			
	Jamaica	1966	30	184	4.05	6.10	19				95	
	Nicaragua	1968–69	74?									
	Uruguay	1966	69	198	2.00	2.50	119	16	16		91	3
	Venezuela	1969	79	205	1.05	2.35		12	7	AB 0.4		0.04?

SOURCES—APPENDIX B

Analysis of debates, except for:

1. Austria: A. Peluka and M. Welan, *Demokratie und Verfassung im Österreich* (Viluha: Europa-Verlag, 1971).
2. Canada: A. Kornberg, "Parliament in Canadian Society," A. Kornberg and L. D. Musolf, eds., *Legislatures in Developmental Perspective* (Durham, N. C.: Duke University Press, 1970), pp. 55–128.
3. West Germany: S. Rothman, *European Society and Politics* (Indianapolis: Bobbs-Merrill Company, Inc., 1970).
4. New Zealand: R. N. Kelson, *The Private Member of Parliament and the Formation of Public Policy* (Toronto: University of Toronto Press, 1964).
5. USSR, Poland, Hungary: M. Lesage, *Les régimes politiques de l'URSS et de l'Europe de l'Est* (Paris: Presses Universitaires de France, 1970).
6. Lebanon: R. E. Crower, "Parliament in the Lebanese Political System," Kornberg and Musolf, *op. cit.*, pp. 273–302.
7. India: *Third Lok Sabha, 1962–67: A Souvenir* (New Delhi: Lok Sabha Secretariat, 1967).
8. Philippines: R. B. Stauffer, "Congress in the Philippine Political System," in Kornberg and Musolf, *op. cit.*, pp. 334–65.
9. Colombia: J. L. Payne, *Patterns of Conflict in Colombia* (New Haven: Yale University Press, 1968).

SOCIAL BACKGROUND AND TURNOVER OF LEGISLATORS

C

Social Background and Turnover of Legislators

	1 Date of information	2 Average age	3 % women	4 Professional (lawyers in brackets)	5 Business	6 Managers	7 Other white collar workers (incl. teachers)	8 Farmers	9 Manual workers	10 Turnover	11 Socioeconomic group of country
Atlantic Area											
Australia	1969	50	0		16	17	24	13	22	24	I
Austria	1970	51	5	8 (8)	12	11	26	2	9	24	I
Belgium	1961			31			6	12			I
Canada	1963		1	56	36	25		2		18	I
Eire	1969		2	30 (26)		3	11	21	8		II
Finland	1970	46	17	15 (14)	16		34	6	3	44	I
France	1968		2	26	7	23	26	11	6		I
Germany, West	1961	49	3	21 (19)			22	1	10	26	I
Italy	1968		4	28 (21)	3	17	36	7	11		II
Luxembourg	1968	52		22 (22)	13		41	27			I
New Zealand	1969	51	5	8 (8)	16		29	15	9		I
Norway	1969	50	9	9	18		43				I
Sweden		47	15								I
Switzerland	1968			18 (18)	12		56	7	8	28	I
UK	1970		4	23 (19)	17	6	34		8	16	I
US	1968		3	51	22		11			15	I
Eastern Europe and North Asia											
Bulgaria	1967		17								II
Germany, East		44	30	22			17	15	44		II
Hungary	1966		20								II
Mongolia	1969		15	4		9	42	25	17		III
Poland	1969		14	6		5	54	15	17		II
Rumania	1966	48	14	19			45	11	20		II
USSR	1969		31			6	44	19	27	48	II
Yugoslavia		48	13	2		53	37	1	1	67	II

Social Background and Turnover of Legislators (continued)

Region	Country	1 Date of information	2 Average age	3 % women	4 Professional (lawyers in brackets)	5 Business	6 Managers	7 Other white collar workers (incl. teachers)	8 Farmers	9 Manual workers	10 Turnover	11 Socioeconomic group of country
Middle East and North Africa	Afghanistan	1969									45	II
	Israel			6							33	II
	Jordan	1968	50		23 (23)	25		43	8			IV
	Lebanon	1968			45 (45)	34	4	15			35	III
	Senegal			1								IV
	Tunisia	1969	45	3	15 (15)	12		43	30			III
	Turkey	1965	43	1	41 (32)	13	10	24	7			III
	UAR	1969	45	1	14 (14)		12	13	18	32		IV
South and Southeast Asia	Ceylon	1970		4								III
	India	1969		6	27 (24)	10	1	32	27	1	60	III
	Japan	1969	55	2		8	28	35	2			I–II
	Philippines	1969		3	74 (74)	15		7	3			III
	Thailand	1969		3	20 (20)	41		4	4	6		IV
	S. Vietnam	1967		2	7 (7)	3		64	3	2		IV
Africa South of Sahara	Botswana	1969	40	4								IV
	Cameroon	1970	30	1	22 (22)	8	6	62			60	IV
	Chad	1969										IV
	Equat. Guinea	1968		6								II–IV
	Ghana	1969	41	1	30 (30)	15	4	30	8	2		IV
	Guinea	1968		21								IV
	Kenya	1969		1					35		63	IV
	S. Africa	1970	52	1	18 (18)	14	2	15				I–II
	Zambia	1968	40	2								IV
Latin America	Chile (Senate)	1969		6	51 (46)	14	16	9	5	5	41 (1961)	III
	Colombia	1970	50	6	66 (66)	12	8	10			77	III
	Costa Rica										100	III
	Dom. Republic	1970		4								IV
	Guatemala										100	IV
	Guyana			11								IV
	Uruguay											III
	Venezuela			2								III

SOURCES—APPENDIX C

Official publications, *or* Interparliamentary Union, *Chronicle of Elections* (Geneva, 1968, 1969, 1970), except for:

1. Austria: A. Peluka and M. Welan, *Demokratie und Verfassung im Österreich* (Viluha: Europa-Verlag, 1971).
2. Belgium: F. Debuyst, *La Fonction parlementaire en Belgique* (Brussels: CRISP, 1967).
3. Canada: A. Kornberg, "Parliament in Canadian Society," in A. Kornberg and L. D. Musolf, eds., *Legislatures in Developmental Perspective* (Durham, N. C.: Duke University Press, 1970).
4. Eire: J. Whyte, "Dail Deputies," *Tuarion Pamphlets*, no. 15.
5. W. Germany: S. Rothman, *European Society and Politics* (Indianapolis: Bobbs-Merrill Company, Inc., 1970).
6. Switzerland: E. Gruner, *L'assemblée fédérole suisse* (Berne: Franche, 1970).
7. Communist countries: M. Lesage, *Les régimes politiques de l'URSS et de l'Europe de l'Est* (Paris: Presses Universitaires de France, 1970).
8. Japan: A. W. Burks, *The Government of Japan* (New York: Thomas Y. Crowell Company, 1961).

SELECTED BIBLIOGRAPHY

As can be expected, textbooks on individual countries normally tend to have a section on the legislature of the country. In this bibliography, we shall refer only to those books (usually written in English) which are specifically devoted to legislatures or to the legislature of the country concerned.

GENERAL WORKS

A. H. BIRCH. *Representative and Responsible Goverment.* London: George Allen & Unwin, 1964.

J. BLONDEL ET AL. "Legislative Behavior: Some Steps Towards a Cross-National Measurement," *Government and Opposition,* V (Winter 1969), 67–85.

LORD BRYCE. *Modern Democracies.* 2 vols. London: Macmillan & Company, Ltd., 1921.

I. D. DUCHACEK. "Parliaments: Rule Modification and Controls," *Journal of Constitutional and Parliamentary Studies* (New Delhi) (January–March 1968), pp. 55–74.

Interparliamentary Union. *Parliaments.* 2nd ed. London: Cassell & Company, Ltd., 1962.

Interparliamentary Union. *Constitutional and Parliamentary Information* (quarterly).

A. KORNBERG AND L. D. MUSLOF, EDS. *Legislatures in Developmental Perspective.* Durham, N. C.: Duke University Press, 1970.

J. LOCKE. *Second Treatise on Civil Government.* 1690.

A. L. LOWELL. *Governments and Parties in Continental Europe.* Cambridge: Harvard University Press, 1896.

W. J. M. MACKENZIE. *Free Elections.* London: George Allen & Unwin, 1958.

BARON DE MONTESQUIEU. *The Spirit of Laws.* 1748.

K. C. WHEARE. *Legislatures.* London: Oxford University Press, 1963.

UNITED STATES

S. K. BAILEY. *Congress Makes a Law.* New York: Columbia University Press, 1950.

J. D. BARBER. *The Lawmakers.* New Haven: Yale University Press, 1965.

LORD BRYCE. *The American Commonwealth.* 3 vols. London: Macmillan & Company, Ltd., 1888.

G. B. GALLOWAY. *The Legislative Process in Congress.* New York: Thomas Y. Crowell, 1953.

M. E. JEWELL AND S. C. PATTERSON. *The Legislative Process in the United States.* New York: Random House, Inc., 1966.

W. J. KEEFE AND M. S. OGUL. *The American Legislative Process.* Englewood Cliffs, N.J.: Prentice-Hall, Inc., 1964.

K. KOFMEHL. *Professional Staffs in Congress.* Lafayette, Ind.: Purdue University Press, 1962.

T. J. LOWI. *Legislative Politics, USA.* Boston: Houghton Mifflin Company, 1965.

D. R. MATTHEWS. *U.S. Senators and Their World.* Chapel Hill: University of North Carolina Press, 1960.

C. MILLER. *Members of the House.* New York: Charles Scribner's Sons, 1962.

R. L. PEABODY AND N. W. POLSBY. *New Perspectives on the House of Representatives.* Chicago: Rand McNally & Co., 1963.

N. W. POLSBY. "The Institutionalisation of the U.S. House of Representatives," *American Political Science Review,* LXII (1968), 144–68.

D. G. TACHERON AND M. K. UDALL. *The Job of the Congressman.* Indianapolis: Bobbs-Merrill Company, Inc., 1966.

D. B. TRUMAN. *The Congressional Party.* New York: John Wiley & Sons, Inc., 1959.

J. C. WAHLKE AND H. EULAU. *Legislative Behavior.* New York: The Free Press, 1959.

J. C. WAHLKE, H. EULAU, H. BUCHANAN, AND LE ROY FERGUSON. *The Legislative System.* New York: John Wiley & Sons, Inc., 1962.

UNITED KINGDOM

A. BARKER AND M. RUSH. *The M.P. and His Information.* London: Faber & Faber, Ltd., 1970.

P. BROMHEAD. *Private Members' Mills in the British Parliament.* London: Oxford University Press, 1956.

P. W. BUCK. *Amateurs and Professionals in British Politics.* Chicago: University of Chicago Press, 1963.

R. BUTT. *The Power of Parliament.* London: Constable & Co., Ltd., 1967.

D. N. CHESTER AND N. BOWRING. *Questions in Parliament.* London: Oxford University Press, 1962.

B. CRICK. *The Reform of Parliament.* London: Weidenfeld & Nicholson, 1964.

R. E. DOWSE. "The MP and His Surgery," *Political Studies* (October 1963), pp. 332–41.

S. E. FINER, H. B. BERRINGTON, AND D. J. BARTHOLOMEW. *Backbench Opinion in the House of Commons.* Long Island City, N.Y.: Pergamon Press, 1961.

A. H. HANSON AND B. CRICK. *The Commons in Transition.* New York: The Fontana Library, 1970.

N. JOHNSON. *Parliament and Administration.* London: George Allen & Unwin, 1966.

H. MORRISON. *Government and Parliament.* London: Oxford University Press, 1954.

A. RANNEY. *Pathways to Parliament.* Madison: University of Wisconsin Press, 1965.

P. G. RICHARDS. *Honorable Members.* London: Faber & Faber, Ltd., 1959.

S. A. WALKLAND. *The Legislative Process in Great Britain.* London: George Allen & Unwin, 1968.

H. W. WISEMAN. *Parliament and the Executive.* London: George Allen & Unwin, 1966.

CONTINENTAL EUROPE

F. DEBUYST. *La fonction parlementaire en Belgique.* Brussels: CRISP, 1967.

P. FERRARI AND H. MAISL. *Les groupes communistes aux assemblées parlementaires italiennes et françaises.* Paris: Presses Universitaires de France, 1969.

E. GUICHARD-AYOUB, C. ROIG, J. GRANGÉ. *Etudes sur le parlement de la 5ème République.* Paris: Presses Universitaires de France, 1965.

D. MACRAE. *Parliament, Parties and Society in France.* New York: The Macmillan Company, 1967.

P. M. WILLIAMS. *The French Parliament.* London: George Allen & Unwin, 1968.

G. LOEWENBERG. *Parliament in the German Political System.* Ithaca, N.Y.: Cornell University Press, 1967.

G. J. DI RENZO. *Personality, Power and Politics* (Italian deputies' attitudes). Notre Dame, Ind.: University of Notre Dame Press, 1967.

E. HASTAD. *The Parliament of Sweden.* Hansard Society, 1957.

E. VAN RAALTE. *The Parliament of the Kingdom of the Netherlands.* Hansard Society, 1959.

E. GRUNER. *L'assemblée fédérale suisse.* Berne: Franche, 1970.

C. J. HUGHES. *The Parliament of Switzerland.* Hansard Society, 1962.

OTHER COUNTRIES

A. KORNBERG. *Canadian Legislative Behavior.* New York: Holt, Rinehart & Winston, Inc., 1967.

N. WARD. *The Canadian House of Commons.* 2nd ed. Toronto: University of Toronto Press, 1963.

S. WEISS AND A. BRICHTA. "Private Members' Bills in Israel's Parliament," *Parliamentary Affairs* (1969–70), pp. 21–33.

R. N. KELSON. *The Private Member of Parliament and the Formation of Public Policy* (New Zealand). Toronto: University of Toronto Press, 1964.

P. H. JUVILER. "Functions of a Deputy to the USSR Supreme Soviet." Unpublished Ph.D. dissertation, Columbia University, 1960.

W. W. MORRIS-JONES. *Parliament in India.* London: Longmans, Green & Company, Ltd., 1957.

The Third Lok Sabha: A Souvenir. New Dehli: Lok Sabha Secretariat, 1967.

H. KANOOR. *Patterns of Politics and Political Systems in Latin America.* Chicago: Rand McNally & Co., 1969.

J. L. PAYNE. *Patterns of Conflict in Colombia.* New Haven: Yale University Press, 1968.

N. M. STULTZ. "Parliament in Former British Black Africa," *Jal. of Devel. Areas* (July 1968), pp. 479–93.

C. GERTZEL. "Parliament in Independent Kenya," *Parliamentary Affairs* (1965–66), pp. 486–504.

R. F. HOPKINS. "The Role of the MP in Tanzania," *American Political Science Review,* LXIV (1970), pp. 754–71.

A. GUPTA. "The Zambian National Assembly," *Parliamentary Affairs* (1965–66), pp. 48–55.

INDEX